The Life
and
Spiritual Journey
of
No One

By R. J. Fidalgo

Copyright © 2023 by R. J. Fidalgo

All rights reserved.

No portion of this book may be reproduced in any form without written permission from the publisher or author, except as permitted by U.S. copyright law.

This publication is designed to provide accurate and authoritative information in regard to the subject matter covered. It is sold with the understanding that neither the author nor the publisher is engaged in rendering legal, investment or other professional services. While the author has used his best efforts in preparing this book, he makes no representations or warranties with respect to the accuracy or completeness of the contents of this book and specifically disclaim any implied warranties of merchantability or fitness for a particular purpose. No warranty may be created or extended by sales representatives or written sales materials. The advice and strategies contained herein may not be suitable for your situation. You should consult with a professional when appropriate. Neither the publisher nor the author shall be liable for any loss of profit or any other commercial damages, including but not limited to special, incidental, consequential, personal, or other damages.

Edition and Revision History

- **First Edition**: Published 2023
- **Second Edition**: Revised and published 2023
- **Third Edition**: Revised and published 2024 (current version)

Cover Art by playgroundai.com

Logo by R.J. Fidalgo

Illustrations by R. J. Fidalgo and @fatimaseehar (Pic. 1,2,3,4 and 5)

This is the **Third Edition, Second Revision, 2024**

Table of Contents

Table of Contents --- 0
    Introduction ... 1
PART ONE - MY LIFE AND JOURNEY --- 3
Chapter One - Childhood --- 5
Chapter Two – Youth and School Life --- 9
Chapter Three – Adolescence to Manhood --- 15
Chapter Four – Spiritual Beginnings --- 25
Chapter Five – The Transcendental Touch --- 31
    Nature - Life and Balance ... 32
    Seeking Answers ... 35
Some Context --- 38
Chapter Six – The First Steps --- 43
Chapter Seven – I Go to India --- 47
    Noida Ashram ... 48
    Ranchi ... 52
    My stay in Kolkata - Dakshineswar ... 56
Chapter Eight – Home Again --- 65
    Sleep ... 66
Dreams and Visions --- 67
A Glimpse of Past Lives --- 68
Chapter Nine – Close Revelations --- 71
Chapter Ten – "Sin" --- 81

Chapter Eleven – The Path -- 85
    Pain and My Personal Dark Night of the Soul.................. 86
    Religion - The Guiding Hand of "God"............................. 88
Chapter Twelve – The Journey Continues (Life & Practice) ----- 91
Chapter Thirteen – The End or a New Beginning ---------------- 101
Chapter Fourteen – Work & My Longing to Help Others ------ 105
    Work 105
    Magic 110
    Hypnosis 112
Chapter Fifteen – Spiritual Cross Road --------------------------- 121
    Struggle - Obstacles and Results 125
Chapter Sixteen – Connecting (Energy, Light & Our Chakras) 127
Chapter Seventeen – Clarity, "Impossibility," Future ---------- 131
PART TWO – THE SPIRITUAL DIET ------------------------- 135
    Introduction... 137
Chapter One - Sex--- 139
Chapter Two - Exercise -- 145
    Finding Middle Ground 146
Chapter Three - Food --- 149
    Key Nutrients - Sources 153
    Deficiencies and Symptoms... 156
Chapter Four - Fasting-- 159
Chapter Five – Ekadashi and Fasting ---------------------------- 163

Fasting and Infection 166

Chapter Six – Gut Health -- 167

Probiotics - Kefir 170

Conclusion 171

PART THREE - UNDERSTANDING ---------------------------- 173

Introduction.. 175

Chapter One – God and The Spiritual World -------------------- 177

Chapter Two – Material Creation---------------------------------- 181

Chapter Three – Divine Mother------------------------------------ 187

Lakshmi 189

Sita and Dharma.. 192

Heroes --- 198

Maya 199

Chapter Four – Lord Krishna (The Mellows) --------------------- 201

The Mellows: 202

The Essence Behind the Mellows -------------------------------- 205

Chapter Five – The Modes of Material Nature (The Gunas) --- 207

Conditioned Souls... 209

Chapter Six – The Yuga's (The Cycles of Time) ---------------- 213

Untangling Concepts... 215

Chapter Seven – The Way Back (Roads of Consciousness) ---- 219

The Third Plane - Choice 224

The Fork in the Road--- 226

Influence -- 227

Important Observations 228

　　　Balance/Healing: Process and Clarification 228

　　　My Final Thoughts 232

　　　Conclusion 235

Appendix I --- 239

Appendix II -- 241

Appendix III --- 243

Appendix IV --- 245

Appendix V -- 247

　　　Bibliography 249

Introduction

I struggled for quite some time with whether to write or not to write this story, this book, about its content, whether I'm worthy of writing it, or if it's of any value to others. I was overwhelmed with a sense of unworthiness, which in turn kept me from moving forward. This feeling of being unworthy is not uncommon, and those who live almost solely in a worldly existence are prone to have it. We should always be humble, but being overly humble only serves to diminish our true selves. I eventually overcame these feelings of unworthiness, but I still believe that my story is no more important than anyone else's. Whatever the story, what is important is that it has led us here and will ultimately lead us to where we need to be. As such, I will make no reference to my name or country; this story could easily be yours, whatever your name or country may be. In much the same way, I consider all spiritual wisdom portrayed in this book not to be my own, and that I'm only the instrument through which it is conveyed.

This world is such a complicated place that I struggled to find a place in it. Everything seemed to weigh heavily on me, but I've come to understand life, this world, and my choice. I always thought that the material and the spiritual were mutually exclusive, but that's not the case. A balance between the two is not only possible but necessary. I've come to find mine. May you come to do the same.

On my journey, there were books, people, and divine souls, whether I was conscious of them or not, and whether they were physical or not, that aided me and are helping me still. So, I write the book of a man from the West on his spiritual journey, with all his struggles, doubts, and difficulties, in hopes that it will help others who are on a journey of their own. If this book succeeds in helping one, I will consider its purpose served.

The Life and Spiritual Journey of No One

PART ONE

My Life and Journey

The Life and Spiritual Journey of No One

Chapter One

Childhood

I was born on the seventh of August in 1978 on a quiet summer night. On that day, my mother-to-be found herself on a stretcher in a hospital hall; as she wasn't in much pain, she waited patiently for the nurse and doctor to call her to the delivery room. After just a little while, all of a sudden, it was over. I remember my mother telling me that she reached out to a passing nurse and said: **"I think he's already out."**

In a family of five, I was the brother to two sisters, one older and one younger than me. My father and mother were educated people with college degrees; they worked in the local school and hospital, respectively, making what one might call an honest living. My mother was, in a way, the sentimental one, and my father the cold practical type. They had their own particular way of parenting. I don't remember my parents playing with me, guiding me, or teaching me much of anything; they were engrossed in their own little worlds, and I was supposed to figure things out for myself. My parents were Christians like their parents before them. They went to church, like so many others, but I never saw them in prayer or heard them talking about such things.

We lived very simple lives. We didn't eat much, and the only meals I truly remember having were lunch and dinner. We had a TV with its meager two channels but scarcely watched it. We rarely entertained guests, only on occasion, and I remember owning just a handful of toys.

Somehow things came to be different for my younger sister, Sara, who was five years younger than me, for whatever reason. We had a nanny who sometimes took care of us, but things were handled pretty much the same way. The exception would be if I stayed overnight; come morning, I would always have breakfast.

I was a very calm and quiet child. I rarely played with my older sister as we seemed to be worlds apart, nor did I play with others. I was mostly alone, playing with the few toys I had, watching history books, or handling a spoon, but often, I was just still and silent for hours, apparently doing nothing. This quietness was so extreme that my parents constantly checked up on me just to ensure I was alive. Usually, they would find me on the sofa or sitting cross-legged in the middle of the room.

My earliest memories were from when I was about four or five years old, and one of my first, if not the first, comes from those moments of quiet and solitude. I distinctly remember thinking: *"What is this? This world isn't right. It's crazy. It makes no sense."* These thoughts came to me often, but I could never figure them out. These were particularly strange thoughts for a five-year-old. What does a child know about the world? Especially one that has little to no interaction with it, directly or indirectly. All I can say is that these thoughts always left me with a powerful feeling of not belonging. This feeling stuck with me all my life, and even though the effects of time diminished its strength, it was never gone, never far from me.

I was also born with a sense of righteousness that ruled my life and made things even harder for me, as they seemed ill-suited for this world, but even so, I always kept them in my heart as precious treasures.

At the age of five or six, something special happened. As far as I can tell, it was a day like any other, my father was cooking or cleaning, and I was alone in the living room. While sitting cross-legged in the middle of the carpet, all of a sudden, I started practicing what I now know to be yogic techniques (35 years later). Unknowingly I was tuning in to the Infinite. I practiced for a while until my father came rushing in.

"What are you doing?" he asked.

I replied, "**Um, nothing.**"

I should have said, "**I have no idea,**" but at that time, that seemed like a reasonable answer to give. I do not know why, but I don't remember doing it again, only returning to it many years later, when I consciously embarked on the spiritual path.

What was interesting about this experience is that through it came the knowledge of a foreign language, English, which somehow I began to speak and understand perfectly. My parents knew little to no English, so the newly acquired knowledge went unnoticed until one day. We were all watching a movie, and as my bedtime approached, they remarked that I might as well go to bed since I didn't understand the narrative. As a kid, I wanted to stay longer and finish the movie, so I said, "**Yes, I do.**" I translated everything word for word, which caught them by surprise, but even so, I went to bed.[1]

On another occasion, my cousins from America came to visit, and I privately and casually started speaking English with them. When my cousins referred to this fact to my parents, they were totally dismissive about it. The power of the Lord to bewilder his children is really something. For a very long time, they did not believe I could have this knowledge, and when they finally did, no importance was given to it (it's quite normal).

As you might have guessed, I wasn't much of a talker, but I never refrained from speaking whenever I felt the need to do so. On one such occasion, I was strolling with my father when we came across a well-dressed gentleman. Something was off about this man, but I couldn't tell what. My father started speaking in a very humorous and pleasing manner, which was completely strange and out of character. As we went on our way, I felt the need to ask:

"**Why were you being so overly nice to that gentleman?**"

He replied in a chastising manner, "**Boy. Stop being a child. In the future, one might need the aid of such persons, so you should always act in a pleasing fashion.**"

---

[1] The film had subtitles which my parents were able to read.

I frowned mildly and thought: *"That doesn't sound right."* I wasn't opposed to treating others nicely, of course, but even at such a young age, I thought it wrong to do so, expecting to profit from it in the future.

Chapter Two

Youth and School life

I always had a fondness for animals, and they seemed to like me too. Often, I would find myself trying to save them, but most of the time, there was little I could do. There was one such event that I will never forget. Our summer vacations were usually spent up North, where we took the opportunity to revisit friends and family members. On one of those summer days, my father and I went to the city to buy car parts. On arrival, my father said, **"Wait next to the car. I'll be back."**

While waiting, a good-looking brown leather dog approached me, it looked like a stray, but I couldn't be sure. I cannot fully convey the joy he expressed upon finding me. He jumped up and down, wagging his tail, rubbing against me, and licking me as if he had found a long-lost friend. I played with him while I could, but soon after, my father arrived with others. The bond between the dog and me was so evident that everyone, except my father, thought the dog was mine.

They remarked, "**Nice dog. Good dog.**"

I replied, "**OK, but he's not my dog.**"

We were about to part for the junkyard in hopes of finding what my father couldn't in the shop, and as soon as we drove away, the dog started running after us. The others said, "**Look, it's your dog.**"

It felt like a scene from a movie or a painting: on a straight road shaded by rows of plane trees, the dog ran desperately, trying to catch up. We must have been going more than 35 mph (almost 60 km/h), but he was keeping up the best he could. In my eyes, he seemed happy. The ride took about five minutes, and I lost track of him in the last stretch, but 30 seconds after we arrived, he came sprinting like an arrow, blazing through the gates toward me. We were all surprised, and my father had an interesting smile on his face. I knew we couldn't keep him—we lived in a small apartment ill-suited for pets—so I said nothing. The junkyard owner said he was looking for a dog to keep, and I was relieved. He would have a place to stay and food to eat, but the dog thought differently and broke free of the collar and chain placed upon him. I wanted no part in confining him, so I let him go. I bind him only in memory.

Soon the time to go to school came, but my parents said very little about it, so much so that I didn't understand what I was doing there or why I had to learn all these things that seemed to me to be so unimportant. I had a tough time in school. I didn't know how to play sports, didn't participate in extracurricular activities, and skipping kindergarten made things worse. Being the silent, lonely type made me even more of a target. Almost every day, someone would try to beat me up. I remember trying not to hurt them too much—just enough to fend them off—but hurting others always made me feel awful, even in self-defense. My parents were completely oblivious to all this, but in their defense, I didn't complain to anyone or show signs of being in a skirmish.

As a side note, and to be entirely truthful, I was once enrolled in an activity. In the third grade, my parents, for some reason that I cannot fathom, enrolled me in ballet, not in any ball-related sports, gymnastics, track, or swimming but in ballet. I was truly a fish out of water and didn't understand what I was doing there. My parents kept me enrolled for three months; after that, I was never enrolled in anything again.

At this point, I started comparing my life to that of other children. I realized that I had nothing they had: no nice clothes or school materials, no activities, no fancy parties or vacations, very few toys, and no friends. I remember thinking: *"I must have a pretty miserable childhood."* In retrospect, I cannot say it was so, I didn't feel unhappy, but I didn't feel happy either. The word that comes to mind is contentment.

On that note, a curious event comes to mind: One day, I was at home waiting for my parents to return. That day was my birthday. There was no plan or setup, but I thought my parents would surely return with cake and a small gift to celebrate (which I envisioned to be a small toy car). First came my mother. She said nothing and went about her business. I thought it strange, but maybe she had arranged things with my father. I stood waiting by the door, and an hour later, he came. He brought nothing and said nothing. They didn't even say "Happy Birthday." What surprised me the most was not the oddness of the situation but how I felt. I completely shrugged it off and said nothing.

In the fourth grade, my father asked my teacher to fail me for some reason. She disagreed but respected his will nevertheless. At the time, I didn't take it very well, but if not for that, I wouldn't have met my very best friend all through adolescence. He was a good, kind person of even mind, and so were his parents. We usually played ball together, explored, took bike rides, and played different games. We were never prone to mischief or ill will against anyone, either in mind or speech. We simply enjoyed each other's company.

I remember he had a pretty good-looking Cocker Spaniel, which I would usually pet and play with. He always seemed happy and playful, but his cheerful manner toward me soon changed due to an interesting event.

I had just arrived at my friend's place, and everyone was quietly having lunch. I saw the dog resting peacefully below the kitchen table, so I crouched down to pet him like I usually did. As I outstretched my hand, he fiercely grabbed it, biting as though chewing on a bone. I stood there quietly and unmoving, watching in surprise for about ten seconds, by which time he let go. I felt no fear, anger, or pain. I was then informed that I had approached a slipper, which he had claimed with serious ownership. I bore no ill will towards the animal and saw what happened as my mistake.

What I found uncanny was that despite my friendly behavior, the animal would growl whenever he saw me. I didn't quite get it, nor did my friend, who found it funny. He stated that the dog got severely punished every time he displayed such behavior and always acted lovingly afterward. This dog was taken in by a loving family, without a doubt. He was used to a certain kind of living, a certain kind of "loving." He could not accept or understand my love for him. This fact brewed fear and suspicion in him, which led to his vicious preemptive growl every time he saw me.[2] I didn't understand it for a long time, but it never made me feel any differently about him.

Later on, my friend and I went our separate ways, but we played our part in each other's lives, and that's what's important. God arranges things in mysterious ways; proof of this has been given to me throughout my life.

I've had quite a few uncanny encounters with animals. Some were more extraordinary than others, but most were of a brighter nature. It would serve no purpose to fill this book with too many of these stories, but there's one that might be worth mentioning due to its unique nature. I don't remember the exact date, but it was a sunny day, and I was leisurely walking home along a dusty road. Suddenly, out of nowhere, I felt an uncontrollable urge to look back. There was no apparent need for it. No one was around, and it was unusually quiet and peaceful. I turned, and as I did, I saw a very large dog rushing toward me with a purpose. The dog was approaching fast, and I intuitively felt that he meant to do me harm. Looking back, I don't believe there was much need for intuition because the dog's expression revealed no other intention than tearing me apart. I felt no fear, and without thought, a natural flow of action led me to raise my foot and stomp it firmly on the ground. The sound and the impressively large resulting wave of dust caused the dog to brake heavily, like in a cartoon. He came as close as seven feet but ended up turning back to run just as fast as he came.

---

[2] This distortion is commonplace in humans, but their severity/complexity ranges greatly as we are indeed more complex life forms. In much the same way, there is a great deal of variety in their outward expressions, ranging from mild to severe. At times this issue may seem to have no apparent cause, but the reason is there. It might just not be from this lifetime.

I was still pretty young, but there was an abundance of events that left me wondering and confused. Often, I would ask myself: "*What was this? Why did this happen? Why did I act in this way?*" There were, of course, answers to these questions, but I couldn't see them at the time.

One day God arranged for me to learn a lesson or to remind me of it. My classmates started noticing that I could fend off anyone that came to do me harm. They began praising and enticing me to fight. Somehow I got bewildered, and pride took hold of me. Soon after, I was looking for a fight and found one. I began to wrestle with the boy that I apparently chose, but he easily threw me down, pinning me to the ground with outstretched arms. I tried to exert force to break free but couldn't, not because he was stronger than me (which he could very well be) but because I had no strength to exert, none. It was gone. Even if he had released my arms, I wouldn't be able to move. After realizing this, I looked at his face. He was so calm and peaceful, and through his gaze came unspoken words:

"***Now you understand.***"

Doing me no harm, he released me. I felt almost immediately that I could move, and we went our separate ways. I came to misuse my gift, and ended up doing what was often painful for me to receive.

Those of good nature who lack in wisdom are prone to fall under less than positive influences. I was made aware of this fact even as a child, but this may play out all through one's life if we let it. Here's another childhood example: I remember leaving school with a group of classmates. My best friend and I were leading, and three others followed close behind. My best friend suddenly found a wallet.

Opening it he said excitingly, "**Look what I found! It's filled with money!**"[3]

Thinking it to be the right thing, I said, "**It's not ours to take. Just let it go.**"

---

[3] This wasn't a lot of money, but for kids like us, it certainly seemed so.

My friend conceded and dropped it on the ground, which was unwise, of course, but what this act set in motion is what I find interesting. One of our group, who was walking just a few paces behind us, found that same wallet.

He opened it and exclaimed with joy, "**It's full of money!**"

Hearing this led others to swarm in like locusts to a crop. My friend was drawn in like the others and said, "**Hey, I found it first, but (name) told me to drop it. Isn't it true?**"

"Yes. That is true," I replied.

My friend then pointed out that it wouldn't be right for him to keep all the money, so after some discussion, someone suggested that the money should be divided equally between us. Somehow I ended up sharing in that ignorance and, as a bonus, got quite the scolding from my friend.

"**That money could have been ours If you just kept quiet.**"

Being a child, I was kind of taken aback. *"How did this happen?"* At the very least, I can say that the wallet did find its way to its rightful owner.

Chapter Three

Adolescence to Manhood

I was a pretty good student all through school, with the exception of one or two subjects, and as it turns out, I was naturally skilled at sports. At this point in my life, I would often ask God: "**What do you want me to do? Am I fated to play this game?**" No answer came, no matter how many times I asked. One day I got tired of asking and said, "**Fine, if you want me to play this game, so be it**." As you can imagine, I said it in a rather angry mood.

Most kids had their rebellious phase that included a whole lot of smoking, drinking, and for a few, sex and drugs. This phase, as it seems, extended for most of their lives. It was always strange for me to see others socializing and trying to fit in by such means, ruining themselves for the sake of belonging. Throughout my life, I made a few attempts of my own at fitting in, but I didn't go through this phase.

I was so confused about what to do that I changed subjects and schools often, both in high school and college. The year before I went to college (age 20), I decided to join a gym. It seemed the logical way to keep myself fit, and I liked the part that you did not have to rely on anyone to do it. At this point, I felt myself becoming more enmeshed in the material world and body. It was in such a place, a year later, that I would meet my partner in life. Although things at one time or another could have gone differently, fate arranged things to play out as they did.

Soon after, I went away to college to study Computer Engineering. As I was going to a faraway city and not knowing anyone, I decided to go along with the rituals applied to first-year students. This school had a severe hazing tradition that went on for a month. First-year students were also obliged to go out every night. The excuse for these practices is the same everywhere in the world, to help students adapt to the school environment, meet new people, and make friends. These are, of course, completely preposterous ideas. How can intoxication, harassment, abuse, and humiliation help you adapt to anything, and what sort of friendship/connection is based on this? Such an experience served to prove, if nothing else, what I already knew. My advice to anyone in a similar situation is not to force things. You will naturally, over time, get to know new people and places without the taint of such things.

The course was very demanding, with challenging subjects, but what took me by surprise was the predisposition of teachers. In subjects like Analytical Mathematics, I don't remember the teacher correcting one exercise fully; he would always stop halfway. In Computer Programming, the teacher actually said that he wasn't there to teach; we had to learn by ourselves. This way of thinking and acting was so bad that the expected time for graduation in a four-year course was eight to ten years. My father wouldn't have any of that, and the following year enrolled me in Biological Engineering back in my hometown. I didn't mind considering what was happening, and I couldn't visualize myself looking at a computer night and day for the rest of my life.

The new school had a well-built structure and very high standards for teaching. Students just had to play the part, which most of them did, with more or less difficulty. Early upon starting, I began to have an interest in bodybuilding. I never wanted to be a muscular monster, but I liked the aesthetics of a few in the "sport."

It surprised me to see what one could do with the body. Ideas of competing naturally started to brew shortly after. I wanted to do what most would consider unthinkable, but I soon realized that a high level of knowledge was required to achieve what I wanted. As a result, I started to study a lot. I was very strict in my doing and didn't deviate. My body became so hungry for nourishment that I didn't pass stool for a month before competing, which was surprising since I was eating six to seven times a day.

One week out from competing, something remarkable happened. I had just finished eating lunch and went to the attic to sit and rest. I sat on the middle of the couch and tried to be comfortable. Shortly after, an indescribable feeling of calm and relaxation came over me. In a split second, I saw myself out-of-body. I seemed like myself, clothes and all, but I was somehow fazed and transparent. My attention then turned to the room, which almost immediately led me to see my body, now an empty vessel, sitting on the couch about ten feet (3 m) away from me. I immediately thought: *"Oh, crap. I'm dead."* That thought got me so scared that my consciousness was thrown back into my body, making me jump five feet from the couch while gasping desperately for air. I kept it a secret for almost twenty years; only recently have I spoken of it and am now writing about it. God was saying in His way: **"Why do you sacrifice so much for this? You are not the body. Can't you see?"**

As it turns out, I wasn't supposed to compete. I relied unnecessarily on others to take me to the show and expected them to be true to their word. Without going into details, I ended up missing the show, which left me in shambles for about a week. I never strived to compete after that, but I continued training and studying nutrition. Eventually, I even tried steroids. I can say that I achieved far better results naturally than with any given drug, but reaching such levels of development and conditioning takes a lot of knowledge and commitment.

In the gym, I befriended many types of people, including bouncers, who eventually introduced me to the world of the night. For most of my college years, I did part-time in discos and nightclubs. The funny thing is that I never socially went or wanted to go to such places. They were loud, dark, filled with smoke, and intoxicated people of various kinds, all very much prone to trouble. Strangely enough, I ended up spending most of my weekend nights in them. I was always invited to work in places where the previous night, someone got stabbed or shot. I always found myself in places where I didn't belong, but throughout my life, I felt protected from those who would harm me, from things I shouldn't do and things I didn't want to do. The coming story illustrates my point exactly.

Picture 1º - Out-of-body experience.

In a city nearby, there is a festival that goes on during winter that lasts three days. At night there was always a party in a large local establishment, and security was always a requirement. The job seemed to pay pretty well for such a short gig, so I accepted an invitation. Shortly after, rumors began to reach my ears about the troublesome nature of this event, and I would soon come to verify them as true. Before continuing, allow me to give some insight about myself: I always saw everybody as the same, men, women, young, old, rich, poor, big and small. I always treated everyone equally, regardless of condition or social status. I always thought everyone should be treated equally and with respect. This also applies to rules. The night my partner and I started working, one of the rules was that no one should enter without a card (paying the fee), and so it was. Almost everyone we interacted with was disagreeable and prone to conflict. The night dragged on when a group of four approached, and the following ensued:

One of the party said, "**This is the chief of the gypsies, and we want to get in?**"

To which I replied, "**Where are your cards?**"

They again said, "**You don't understand, this is the chief, and we are his men?**"

I then emphasized, "**I understand, now where are your cards?**"

More of their men came as we went back and forth in our conversation. At that point, the chief pulled me aside and placed his arm around my neck. I promptly brushed him off, which led us to gaze at each other fiercely, much like a standoff. I remember thinking that conflict was unavoidable. My partner then came, pulled me aside, and said, "**It's alright now.**"

One of their men went to pay for the entries, and we let them pass. I remember my partner's anxious words: "**I only have three bullets.**"

I can say that these were very long nights, and I would see that same gang every time. They were surprised to see me back night after night and seemed to know an awful lot about me, which was odd and uncomfortable. A week later, I was hitching a ride with an acquaintance from work, and he heard of my strife with the chief. He informed me that the chief was always armed and asked if I knew what had happened to him.

I said, "**No. What happened?**"

He replied, "**He was in a car accident. He's in pretty bad shape, full of casts, and with all his teeth knocked out.**"

At that moment, I was convinced that this was the work of providence. I never heard from them again.

Upon writing this story, a dream revealed what later scripture confirmed. God gives divine protection to His devotees, and those who transgress against them or seek to benefit from it, directly or indirectly, are condemned to suffer for many lifetimes. Those who walk in virtue are indeed protected by those of light but do not take this truth as a free pass to be reckless or dismissive. You are not shielded from "life," be wise in your doing, and do not tempt "fate," for your actions have very real consequences.

As you can imagine, the world of the night wasn't the best environment. Nor did it bring the best company, so I ended up falling into ignorance yet again. Under the influence of others and bewildered by faulty reasoning, I did "wrong," but mostly to myself.

Of one such friendship, I had a really tough time letting go. I knew he wasn't the best influence. He was conditioned that way, but I would often find myself overlooking behavior that I would never accept in anyone else. I would usually say to myself: *"He's not that bad. At times, he is good. Sometimes, he acts right."* Only through the hand of God many years later did I come to be free.

I graduated from college with good grades and soon started looking for work. I had a few jobs in my field: research assistant, quality manager, teacher, and consultant, but after much tribulation, I decided to change and become a fitness instructor/personal trainer. At about this time, my son was born. This pregnancy was mostly planned by my partner in life. News of the fact, I remember, took me by surprise. We weren't married then, and I was unsure about the idea of having children, and I'll explain why.

My parents were miserable, constantly arguing and being unpleasant to each other. Family life overflowed with negativity, and kids were collateral damage. All I saw were dysfunctional families all around me, falling apart or already broken. Few were the exceptions. Marriage is a serious commitment, and I wondered: *"If this is the reality for most, who am I to say I'll be any different."* No one should be obliged to live a life of misery, husband or wife, nor should they impose it on others.

On the other hand, divorce always inflicts a heavy toll on children, who need the nourishing/educating figures of father and mother. The only thing left for me to do at this point was to be the best parent I could and raise him right. However, what this implies is now commonly distorted by most. Parents have the duty and responsibility of educating and protecting their children. These are vital points that are often neglected and misunderstood. Parents tend to shield their children from anything and everything, in a sense that the child "never" feels the consequences of their own "wrong" doing. At times this is so extreme that the child doesn't even know that a certain action is "wrong," much less the harmful effects that come with it. The parents act under the false idea that they are doing right or good, which is not true. You are depriving the child, the soul, of learning experiences that would possibly prevent it from harming himself and others in this life and lives to come.

Don't hinder your children in this way. Don't hinder yourselves. As parents, you have your own lessons to learn; try to play the part. I digress, and for that, I am sorry, but I couldn't help but emphasize the responsibility one shoulders when deciding to play the role of parent.

When I started working for a friend in the fitness world, I was expecting good things. To be in a good environment for body and mind. To work in something I really liked and help others. As it turns out, I was expecting too much, and it was just more of the same. This was no ordinary gym. It was guided by strict rules and discipline; I have nothing against such things. They are just a way of instilling habit, but we had more than most; many were entirely out of place and disproportionate. More often than not, late-night meetings were scheduled to rearrange things, demand more, or reproach us in one way or another. I would usually remain silent despite not agreeing, for I understood that any objection to what was being said would be pointless, regardless of any fine reasoning behind it. We had a really good team in place, but there never was a good working environment, which was kind of a shock. It was like we were all struggling to push through, and as time went by, we struggled more.

Part of the job prescription was to "enforce" the rules of conduct within the gym, which was fine by me, if I wasn't the only one earnestly striving to "enforce" them. This fact led to unpleasant situations, as one would expect from a place roaming with large egos. Rather than helping out, my teammates would usually approach me and say in a cautionary fashion, "**Look, that guy is a judge.**", "**...the chief of police.**", "**...special forces.**", "**...the president.**", "**...a doctor.**", "**...a millionaire.**", "**...a champion.**" or whatever. Like this would condition me to act differently somehow. I knew not what they did, what they accomplished or gained in this world, nor did I care. How they behaved was the only thing that mattered, everyone was the same to me.

Similarly curious was when someone endeavored to reveal the identity of a certain someone by the car they owned or through the one they dated/married. For me, these efforts were fruitless, but everyone else always seemed to know exactly who they were talking about.[4]

The job was pretty demanding, and so was my employer. Nothing was ever good enough. The more I did, the more I needed to do. I was even chastised for doing exactly what I was told to do. Foreseeing the near future, I spoke out. Despite knowing it to be futile, I had to say what needed to be said. My input wasn't very well received, and things got a little out of hand, but I do not regret trying to do what was right.

I've learned that the world of work can be a hazardous, crazy place, like a box full of surprises. I've been fired for doing my job, overworked, underpaid, unpaid, etc. I always strived to be honest, hardworking, and pro-

---

[4] Common expressions like "my girlfriend" or "my wife" were always strange and foreign to me. They always seemed to carry the weight of ownership with them. Do people purposely express themselves with such intent? I do not know, but such words always seem to convey something binding. If I use such words in this book, I do so solely for the sake of narrative, nothing more.

fessional, but such things seemed to hold little value in the world. I always did everything with the utmost care and attention. To me, no form of work/service should ever be addressed neglectfully, whatever it may be.

My predisposition often led others to portray me as a perfectionist, which is not true. I just try to do everything to the best of my ability, which is often far from perfect. I always try my best and working for me or others, paid or not, made absolutely no difference. Although strange for most, this was something engraved in the very core of my being. I was subconsciously led to act by the understanding that all forms of work/service, be it to yourself or others, are just a way, an opportunity to express love.

After realizing that I couldn't expect much from working for a friend, I decided to quit my job and stop working for others. I thought long and hard about what I was going to do next. For a while, I thought about opening my own company, but having others doing my bidding for profit never sat right with me. On the other hand, discord always brews between employer and employee. Why would I think that with me, things would be any different? As such, I decided to become a trader.[5] I knew nothing about it but decided to learn. This was quite an endeavor, and to be honest, I still struggle with it. Is this what I'm supposed to do? I then decided to stray from the pattern of society and live a simpler life, just to have what we need, not what we think we need or want. One may not make much money, but one may not need it also, as it turns out, we became happier and happier.

---

[5] Someone who endeavors to make a living through the act of buying or selling stocks, bonds, currency, or other commodities.

The Life and Spiritual Journey of No One

Chapter Four

Spiritual Beginnings

Two years passed, and even though I was happier, something was missing, but I didn't know what. I tried to fill that hole with practical knowledge, but I was never satisfied. At this point, I traveled abroad to care for my sister, who was set to undergo surgery. Sara was the spiritual one, constantly endeavoring to learn something new in the field of spirituality, but I never paid much attention to it. Aside from taking care of my sister, I wanted to take that opportunity to revisit a master, a Chinese mystic. I had met him about a year ago. I remembered my sister dragging me to Chinatown, insisting that I meet this man.

I was somewhat dismissive about the encounter, but this master astrologer predicted a few things that came to pass, which impressed me. Since arrangements were already made for me to return, I was set in my mind to see him again and do things seriously. Somehow, he remembered me from before, which somewhat surprised me, and I handed him my birth certificate.

I said, **"Look, I want to take things seriously this time around, so let's start anew from the beginning."**

He replied, **"OK, let me just check the hour of your birth."**

Saying this, he left the building and went outside. I was puzzled, wondering what he was doing. Was he consulting the Sun, the wind, or something else? All I know is that he came back five minutes later, saying, "**This number is very, very accurate.**"

He spoke about many things, but I will only reveal what I feel is relevant at this point. He described scenes from my past as though they were playing out before him and laughed. He then started sharing what was to come.

Mystic – "**At age 40, you will become much more spiritual.**"

I thought it strange but considered it to be a good thing.

"**You are going to be sick, very, very sick. Wow...**" He sat upright and very attentively focused. He then laughed mildly and said, "**You're going to be OK.**"

I was surprised and later learned that this was no normal sickness.

"**Never change your plan. NEVER. Someone will try to take it from you.**"

"**You are going to do Yoga.**"

Me – "**YOGA???**"

I thought: *"Me, the hard-core fitness guy doing yoga, seriously."* We both looked at each other and laughed dismissively. "**Ha, ha, ha.**"

We both had little understanding of what Yoga really was and thought of the physical aspect and its exercises, which had nothing to do with me.

Mystic – "**I see you traveling to the East, somewhere on the Indian ocean.**"

For about an hour, he talked, and I listened. As we parted ways, he glanced at me in the most gentle and peaceful way, which I couldn't understand at the time. Later on, I checked for locations on the map, but there was no country I wanted to visit—far from it. With my sister almost fully recovered, a week later, I returned home and continued with my regular routine in life.

One day, I stumbled into an interview with a former bodybuilding champion. He went through an existential crisis that led him to a spiritual quest for meaning. That search drove him deep into a tropical jungle. There, he met a shaman priest who brewed a sacred drink of foul taste and extraordinary properties—Ayahuasca. I was intrigued. This was quite out of character.

As a man of science, I did my research. This brew was made of sacred plants that held a compound named DMT. This compound is produced in the human body and is released in large quantities at the time of death. I heard about extraordinary experiences narrated by mathematicians, biologists, chemists, and philosophers. The nature of these varied greatly, and some were rather unpleasant, which intrigued me even more. After more research about the plant, I decided to commit myself to finding and brewing it.

With some effort, I managed to attain the plants in question. Preparing this was no easy feat. It demanded close and constant supervision not to overheat, yet required continuous boiling without singeing the compound. Any distraction would render the brew useless. This whole process took about twelve hours.

By evening, I was ready to drink the concoction, but not without wearing a diaper. Yes, the part about a diaper surely caught your attention. It might not be common, but there is a possibility of losing control over bodily functions, leading to an unpleasant release of stool and urine in your pants.

Drinking the brew and keeping it in was quite a task. I don't know how paint thinner tastes, but I imagine it would be something like this. Just thinking about it brings its taste and smell to mind—not in a good way. I went to lie down in bed and waited. After a while, a numbness paired with a tingly feeling grew up from my feet. Suddenly, I couldn't move. My breath was fading. I was fighting for minutes, gasping with increasing difficulty at the small amounts of air I could, and then I thought:

"Well, I'm dying. It's my own fault. Just let go."

As soon as I did, I was gone. Geometric shapes of different colors appeared before me, and then I was enveloped by an earthy muck—dark and suffocating, though not in a physical way. I was struggling upward, trying to break free, which I did. Above ground, a great tree stood before me, and I could see the life force running within it. It seemed to branch out from the ground, giving me a feeling of connectedness.

After that, I was transported in consciousness through wormholes—tunnels filled with irregular breaches of light. I was sent at great speed to many places, many of which I can't remember. Right after "awakening," a forgetfulness took over me, but I will try to relate as much as I can.

I saw ancient Egypt and the eye of Ra—or should I say of Horus—which I later found out was an exact replica of the pineal gland in the brain. I was also sent to the ancient civilizations of Central and South America. I saw more than one, but I'm unable to say which ones (Maya, Aztec, Inca). Despite not knowing the full history of these civilizations, I can say they played a vital role in Earth's development.

Many would agree these were advanced cultures, but my meaning extends to the metaphysical. In ways I cannot fully fathom, they elevated overall human consciousness to where it is today.

After this, I saw other planets with structures of light radiating in daytime, like great cities at night. At a certain point, an entity appeared. All I could see were its titanic eyes—bright red, gazing at me, filling me with fear. My teeth couldn't stop shaking.

After a while, I was sent away and saw myself before a blazing light. A gentle smile was on my face, and I felt happiness and comfort. This was the last thing I saw and felt before regaining "consciousness."

The experience lasted four hours. The conventional notion of time was gone. I saw so many things—most of them I can't even describe, and others I don't remember. I was so tired. My brain felt like it was an inch from burning out. The best way I can describe it is as if each and every neuron in my brain were firing unceasingly, simultaneously, from beginning to end. I realized that if it lasted any longer, I would suffer damage or death.

This experience stirred something within me, even though unconsciously. I strived to relive it a year later and yet again later on, but to no avail (nothing). I finally understood that this was not the way. In my case, I didn't know any better. I knew nothing about spiritual things or practices, but this reminded me how people often strive to achieve their goals to no cost to themselves, putting little to no effort at all, and if someone can give it, all the better. Sadly, for them, such things do not exist.

Life went on, and so did the hole I couldn't fill. I decided to change my diet and started on Keto. I reduced eating from six to three times a day and even started fasting. My body took a very long time to adapt to the new diet—six months—far more than most, but since I didn't have any hormonal or organ dysfunctions, I stuck to it. As long as I know I'm doing things right, I don't mind facing difficulty.[6]

---

[6] The Keto diet holds its foundation on fats. In other words, 70-80% of your daily food intake is fat, and despite what you might be thinking, it's a pretty healthy diet if done properly. However, I do not believe that this is something for life.

The Life and Spiritual Journey of No One

Chapter Five

The Transcendental Touch

It was the beginning of summer, and I was about to turn 40. On this particular day, I was sitting quietly on the couch, gazing at nothing, when suddenly something happened. I would describe it as a pain filling and bursting through my chest, but it was not exactly a pain. It felt wonderful. A realization and liberation from things that were unconsciously binding me ensued. For the next three to four months, it continued, at times filling me with a deep sense of peace, love, and clarity. For some reason, I couldn't bear to watch TV or listen to the radio. The only thing I could tolerate was spiritual music, and somehow I was drawn to listen again and again.

Moreover, a curious drive for atonement and forgiveness began to overwhelm me, so much so that I even tried to bestow it on someone I thought wronged me in the past. Thankfully, providence protected me from acting out such folly. Atonement and forgiveness do not hinge on the thoughts, words, and acts of others. How would you feel if your efforts were rejected by another? How would this affect your process? True atonement is an unwavering will to do what's "right" from there on out. It rests only on you, much like forgiveness. We tend to seek them from without, but such things lie only within, whether it be for yourself or for others.

One time, for a few moments, a most beautiful experience was given to me. It was in the most trivial circumstance that held no significant weight, but it sprouted a response that didn't come from me—or so it seemed. I was acting and speaking but with no thought. No sense of self was present. It poured through me with no taint or resistance. Such indescribable freedom—I cannot properly put it into words, but I will never forget it.

Nature - Life and Balance

After such an experience, it's not uncommon to develop newfound love and respect for all life. Some are already born with it, and my "experience" just heightened what was already there. This phenomenon may express itself in extreme forms, like refraining from stepping on grass, which in turn leads others to label them as crazy. I do not believe such individuals to be crazy, just overwhelmed, lacking in balance and understanding. In my case, I was fortunate enough to find both quickly.[7]

We were meant to create and interact with the world in a deeper, higher sense, and we should always strive to do so in a wise, balanced fashion. I seek not to kill any "bug" that finds its way into my home; I often try to reallocate them to where they should be. Some might consider this strange, but I believe it to be a cleaner, wiser, and more balanced way of acting.

"Unfortunately," this world is conceived in such a way that, at times, such things are not possible. I always strive to prevent such situations, but they inevitably tend to occur. I will give some examples to illustrate:

My cat lives at home on the third floor. He never goes outside, but somehow he still manages to catch fleas. I bear no ill will, but I must safeguard my pet's health as well as my own. Let's take lice as another example. You can do things to prevent these pests, but even so, you or your children may still catch them. If shaving your head is not an option, then deal with them

---

[7] In this regard, at least, because proper balance in all things would come much later.

you must. Remember that cleanliness is next to godliness, and this applies to house, body, and mind.

There are those who profess more natural forms of living. Some deny specific forms of scientific advancement, while others deny many. Some live in the wild; others eat only raw foods, etc. In sum, this idea can express itself in many forms, and most of them are ultimately binding. I agree that we should live a more balanced existence, and communing with nature is indeed a part of it, but such ways of thinking and doing are, more often than not, a denial of the gifts given to man.

The intellect was given to face the challenges of life. Why not use it to build better shelter, clothing, transportation, medical care, food, etc.? Indeed, these things should be for the profit of all mankind, but often they only seem to flow if they profit the agenda of a few. My intent is not to challenge the choices of others. Do as you will; just make sure to have sound reasoning behind them.

My predisposition toward nature changed, but so did nature's predisposition toward me. I found that animals were particularly sensitive to the phenomena I was experiencing. My cat was such an example. He started displaying the most uncanny behavior. He would purr loudly, stand, and rub his head against my own—against my hands—for hours. The first time, I endured it, but the next time, I didn't indulge as much. I remember thinking:

"Animals aren't meant to be confined in cages or houses. We do so and play with nature to satisfy our wants and whims without regard for the consequences."

Yes, taking in a pet can be good, but those with good intentions often fall into "error." Many take hold of strays, not to adopt them, but with the expectation of delivering them to a shelter or that someone else will take them in. However, we usually fail to understand that when we take hold of an animal, we immediately accept the possibility of taking it in ourselves. I've seen mistakes like these made many times, and I've made them myself, but the worst is when you force those decisions on others.

Some examples of this can be given. For instance: Couples often take in pets, usually not out of a consensual want but to indulge one of the parties. What ends up happening is that often these relationships break, and one of them might end up with a pet they didn't really want in the first place. Another example is senior citizens taking in pets they know might outlive them. In such a case, the responsibility of taking care of these pets might fall on their children, who might not welcome the role. In either of these cases, like in so many others, these individuals will find themselves in a complicated situation that will drive them to act in certain ways. Such things should not be forced or imposed on others, whether they are your parents, children, friends, strangers, or whoever. Who they are doesn't matter; the karmic entanglement is the same—for you and for them.

The examples I have given are of a particular type. Still, in a general sense, I would like to advise those of a kind/loving nature to endeavor to become wise lest they bring "trouble" to themselves and others. It saddens me to see so many good, loving souls with the inability to cope with this world. Many will develop mental disorders; others will become hypocritical, and a few will even find themselves enveloped by darkness. I believe that some wisdom and understanding would go a long way in relieving the strain on these souls, but the world seems poorly arranged to make it so.

Seeking Answers

A month passed since the beginning of the phenomena, and I started thinking to myself:

"What is this? Where does it come from? I don't want to lose it. How can I keep it forever and make it stronger? I cannot be the only one in the world to have experienced this."

This set me on a mission to find out. I had never read so much in such a short time. Until then, I was only interested in reading about science and practical things I could use in life. I went through many books and realized the phenomena to be Cosmic Consciousness - God.[8] I could relate to the experiences of many who were touched in that very same way, but the answer to the most crucial questions still eluded me: How can I keep it forever? How do I make it stronger?

I found so many souls touched in so many beautiful ways, but I was surprised to see that very few were driven to find the what, the how, or the why behind these experiences. I had experienced so many things in life, but I believe that most were not meant to be a definite **wake-up call**. Different things do indeed work for different people, but many times, not even "harsh" or "extraordinary" experiences come to move those who have them. Most of the time, we remain asleep, unconscious in our own way of living.

I've come to know quite a few stories over the past few years, but those who piqued my interest were the ones on opposite ends of the spectrum. Those who seem to be spiritually driven by every "fleeting" thing, and those moved by nothing at all, no matter the grade of experience in question. I was especially interested in the latter. These stories are not mine to tell, but I was often baffled by the apathy of those who had them. No matter what, they cared not to believe, understand or accept.

---

[8] The Name, Word - God, arouses a number of different feelings in different people, and more often than not, these feelings tend to be of a negative nature for several reasons. I recognize this truth, but the word - God, is a widespread concept recognized by many in this world. As such, I cannot refrain from using it from time to time.

I came to realize that we are all spiritually driven to seek by different things in different ways, but others have different paths in life. We just have to accept it, no matter how close we are to them. I might say that I felt more highly driven at a particular point, but my way of seeking, my path is just that, mine. Others will surely find and have more suitable paths/ways elsewhere.

My search continued for a while until I came across the book that spoke to my soul: "***Autobiography of a Yogi***" by Sri Paramahansa Yogananda. Through the words of a yogic master, I finally found what I was seeking. At this time, I was still in a state of wakefulness, and even before finishing the book, I started making my first efforts at meditation. My attempts were short and feeble, but my efforts were nevertheless acknowledged by way of a gift. It was given in bed soon after practice. It felt like an invisible hand was pushing the corners of my lips into a smile and holding them there. I was relishing the moment, but I couldn't help reaching out to touch whatever force was doing it, but of course, I couldn't. Soon after, it was gone.

These signs are given to many, and they differ in nature. They are often uncomprehended and dismissed by beginners, but they do not fail to leave a longing in the heart of the ones who have them. At a certain point, I became aware of a curious phenomenon. The place I chose to do my short meditations had gained some sort of strange magnetism. Compasses went screwy at that exact spot. Over time this phenomenon evolved to what appeared to be a shift in magnetic North. I was puzzled for quite some time, but in time I came to understand its meaning, as will probably all of you.[9]

After finishing the book, I applied for lessons at Self-Realization Fellowship. Meanwhile, I felt the need to do something, maybe speak to someone who was in a better place than me. My sister Sara, who was on vacation at the time, suggested I speak with a certain woman who, by coincidence or not, lived in my hometown. I came to know her as a mystic belonging to the order of the Templars. She was known to guide others through their struggles in life, and so on the eighth of August, we met, and the following ensued:

---

[9] The shift was about 19 to 20° East.

Mystic – **"You have to follow the spiritual path. You have no choice."**

Me – **"No kidding. But I'm so old. How can I reach the goal that some fail to achieve in a lifetime?"**

Mystic – **"I see your spiritual master with you and don't worry, you will live to be a very old man."**

I thought to myself: *"I don't know if I should consider this good or bad news."*

"You will achieve enlightenment in two years, but you must do many things first. You have to be initiated by someone connected to Master Yogananda."

Me – **"Initiated by who?"**

Mystic – **"You haven't met him yet. You will go to India in February and spend a whole month there."**

Me – **"OKKK."**

Mystic – **"You will feel at home, which will be strange. You will meet a man there who will be like a father to you. This man will help you and initiate you."**

"You will open a center or an ashram for yoga in two years. You will bring a different energy and lead by example".

I was not very much convinced. *"How would I accomplish such a thing? How could I sustain such a place?"*

"Are you thinking of having another child? You have someone waiting for you, a little girl."

Me (I sighed and said) – **"Look, I have a really troublesome child. Only through great effort have I been able to keep it together. I cannot possibly handle another."**

Mystic – "But this is a soul of pure light. Let me see what the problem is with your son. Is his grandfather still alive?"

Me – "Not the one on the mother's side."

Mystic – "He is here next to your son. He doesn't want to harm the child but is prone to create chaos and discord."

Me – "Well, that's definitely not good... He was a very troubled soul who inflicted pain on others and ended up committing suicide."

Mystic – "Don't worry; we will help him, but you must do your part."

Me – "OK, if it's to help the boy, I'll do it."

A few more things transpired in our meeting, but they are of no consequence or interest. At this point, I have to fill you in on a few facts/events that are relevant to the story before continuing.

Some Context

There are a few places in the world that I would never consider going to. One such place, as it happens, was India. It was right up there with Afghanistan, Pakistan, Libya, Syria, and Iraq. I would more easily go to Antarctica than any of the places mentioned above. I always had a persistent feeling that I would die, and that impression stuck with me. Still, at this particular point in time, I was willing to go anywhere, and remembering the words of the Chinese mystic, I knew I was due to travel East. I booked the flights the very next day. I was set to leave on the first of February and return on the twenty-fifth. I didn't want to act like a puppet, so I chose not to leave at the end of the month. I thought: *"I still have free will."*

I didn't have a place to go or stay, and I didn't care. I would live on the street if I had to. People thought I was kidding, but I really wasn't. At this point, I hadn't even started the lessons, so I was pretty much clueless about everything. Only a week later, I thought: *"OK, where can I go? Where should I stay?"* I saw that there were ashrams in India where devotees could stay, so I chose three in a random order, or so I thought (Noida, Ranchi, Dakshineswar). Without contacting the ashrams to make arrangements or even knowing their location in the country, I booked the flights. Somehow, the flights were in the proper order, the time I was allowed to stay in each ashram was just right, and it coincided with things I had to see and attend. I was so eager in my mind that I didn't pay attention to anything. It was like throwing bricks and cement into the air and somehow ending up with a perfect wall. I didn't even have a traveling visa at the time. Truly, a divine arrangement.

Family

The subject of my son, which I'm about to address, branches out into three more: my wife, daughter-to-be, and rogue souls. In this life experience, I always tried to avoid anything related to ghosts, possessions, black magic, and other similar things. I was utterly oblivious to them. I was so engrossed in my material existence that I cared not to know or deal with them apart from the occasional horror movie, but fate ordained otherwise. It's been almost 19 years since I've been with my wife. I knew early on that her father took his own life when she was about seven and that family life was plagued with violence and death threats.

I know little about the details of all this, but her father was a troubled person prone to intoxication that brewed a deep anger that hid within him. My wife was sheltered from most of this. Her older sister (14 years older) took it upon herself to do what the mother couldn't and protected her the best she could. So as you can imagine, family life was difficult, especially for those who were very much aware of their circumstances.

When my son was born, he was, by all accounts, a normal child. As the years went by, my wife and her mother often said that they saw the grandfather in him and that the child would often be violent toward them both. I would completely dismiss it until the first time I got a glimpse of it. One day, when he was about three, we were alone in the living room. He was facing me quietly, sitting on the couch. Suddenly, his face turned like something out of a horror movie. A deep, disturbing cry reflected an overflowing rage. I was stunned in surprise, but almost automatically, out of nowhere, I slapped him sideways, two or three times (on the bum and thigh). Right after that, it was gone. His face turned quiet and serene. Not a whisper came out of him, which I thought odd since I slapped him somewhat hard.

I didn't know what to do about a situation I didn't understand, and as time passed, I came to forget it. The mystic brought it back from memory, and we tried our utmost to help, but the results were scanty at best. In all fairness, I must say that the episodes became lighter and more spaced out but never really gone. The first cause was the boy, who was extremely sensitive and receptive. The second was his mother, whom I came to recognize as the anchor to her dead father.

That seven-year-old girl, my wife, never let go of her father. There were hints about this. I just didn't pay any attention. The list of memorabilia was crazy. She even stored away **72 bottles** of spoiled liquor, the very same thing that caused so much grief. This attachment might seem irrational, but we have to look at this through the eyes of a sheltered child:

Before performing the act, her father went to say goodbye the only way he knew how. The means to that end was a rare act of play shared between them. No words were spoken. Only tears sprouted from the depth of his despair.

The result was a seven-year-old child feeling responsible for her father's death: *"If only I had said something. If only I had said the right words."* We often wish we acted differently on such and such occasions, but this is foolish thinking. If we had acted differently in the past, we would've been different people than we actually were. On the other hand, there would be no guarantee of achieving the desired result. In all certainty, no words or actions could have erased what was so deeply rooted within.

It seems to me that we are all broken in some way or form and that this world is poorly arranged to change that fact. In my way of thinking, I never saw bringing souls into this world as a proper way of service. Quite the opposite. If anything, true service would be to keep them away from this "madness." However, things are not so simple, and those who are set to come will come through me or through others. Realizing this fact did not change how I felt, and what's waiting for those who come is still the same.

So as you can see and understand, having a second child was ultimately out of the question, much like going to India, but the time was ripe for these things to be. I could not have acted any other way.

The Life and Spiritual Journey of No One

Chapter Six

The First Steps

Before that blessed state left me and I truly began on the spiritual path, I was guided to **Lord Krishna** and the ***"Bhagavad Gita."*** It spoke of things I've always sensed to be true, and the connection I felt to Krishna was yet to be explained. It was like Truth was being shown to me, along with a way to get there, through Paramahansa Yogananda.

As I feared, that blessed state of being finally parted from me. I realized it was now the time to do my part and travel the road ahead. I will not try to sugarcoat what came next, for it wouldn't benefit anyone. As such, I will try to disclose everything to the best of my ability and in the proper order. My intention is not to instill fear but to help those who go through similar ordeals.

A great heaviness started to fall upon me. It felt like something was trying to crush me. Everything weighed heavily, from the clothes on my back to the strands of hair on my shoulders. Along with it came pain and stiffness all day and night. I would usually wake up worse, that is, if I managed to sleep anything at all. This was so bad that despite my best efforts to relax and stand up straight, I would most likely be looking like the hunchback of Notre Dame.

At times I would be plagued by disturbances of the gut and stomach, and my energy would be faint and weird. I didn't know where this was coming from, but often, I would have to lie down and rest. At a certain point, even vertigo appeared.

My nights were terrible. I was so tense and restless that I had little to no sleep. For a time, I thought the problem might be the mattress or the pillow. I bought two very expensive pillows thinking one of them might do the trick, but no. I tried sleeping in different places, but that didn't work either. Finally, I realized that the problem wasn't the accessories but me. I just had to live through it.

My mind had no rest. I was constantly attacked by terrible thoughts that varied in nature: sex, violence, stealing, cheating, ideas of glory, and grandeur.

"Where did they come from? I never had such thoughts. How come I have them now? Shouldn't my mind be dwelling on goodness, on higher things?"

Those who seek to follow the light are often targets. Darkness sees them as disruptive to their ways, so they strike in whatever way they can. The brighter the light, the more it will inadvertently feel the weight of its polar opposite. One can come to suffer from various degrees of affliction, which can be physical, mental, or spiritual. However, I came to see the spiritual as the worst kind.

Meditation became extremely difficult. I was so restless I could hardly describe it. I could find no posture to sit in, always conscious of the pains in my body. Only through extraordinary effort could I remain still. Behind closed eyelids, my eyes were blazing in a thousand directions. It was crazy. I remember trying different seats and even cutting a few down. Finally, I had one built, but nothing really changed. The few things that always helped a little were drinking a full glass of water upon waking up, brushing my teeth, and clearing the airways before practice. Despite all my difficulties, I never shied away from my duties. I always thought:

"Lord, a little pain and suffering will not turn me away from Thee."

At this point, I was susceptible to mental and spiritual afflictions. If I mistakenly did wrong, thinking it to be right, I would inadvertently suffer great pain and distress. Relief would only come if I stopped trying or made amends of some sort. Such moments were always unbearable to me. Thankfully, they were few in number.

One such occasion was when I was trying to solve an issue regarding a bank account of my mother's. I explained the situation more times than I can remember, each one more stressful than the other. After going to the bank for the third time and accomplishing nothing, I started to get the picture, but the Lord wanted to make sure. We were returning home, about five minutes out when the feeling of getting a parking ticket came to mind. On arrival, there it was. The conspicuous note sticking out from the windshield of my poorly parked car. My father mentioned that the police officer was there not five minutes ago. Later that day, I went back to my parents, gave them the papers, and said, "**Look, figure things out amongst yourselves. I really don't care. I want nothing to do with it.**" After that, I was fine.

I always strove to study and follow the teachings in the lessons, but I found even the simplest practices so hard to execute. It seemed that at every turn, all I saw were obstacles. Upon starting the energization exercises, things took a turn for the worse. Execution of these exercises implies tensing and relaxing, but I was never relaxed to begin with. It ended up building up more stiffness in my body. When I started the Hong-Sau technique about a month before my departure, I finally saw some calmness in my practice. Notwithstanding, my ordeals remained the same, and meditation was still very hard. I had many doubts about my practice, and no one in authority to clear them. I had no choice but to be patient.

Besides the practices given, I intuitively started performing a few others: silence, fasting, chanting, praying at meals, and adequately offering obeisances, which I came to find curious. I was almost a full-fledged vegetarian, only eating fish on occasion, something I thought I'd never do. Curiously, being silent was much more difficult than I expected. Only after many attempts did I really succeed. I would usually fall prey to the environment's stimuli. I was earlier conveyed this fact through a dream, the only pleasant dream I had before departing:

It was a bright clear day, and I looked like a Franciscan monk living in an abbey. I was working in the fields collecting vegetables. Next to me was someone that seemed to be my superior, but this was more a feeling than anything else. Suddenly I stood holding a bundle of vegetables and asked, "**Where should I put them?**"

I realized I'd just broken a vow, and in surprise, placed my hand over my mouth. Affectionately the monk looked at me and smiled. I saw that this practice was not as easy as it seemed and that I shouldn't feel too bad for failing.

Chapter Seven

I Go to India

The time to depart was fast approaching, but the desire to go was gone. The trip made no sense in my mind. There were no logical answers to my questions. *"What am I doing? Why am I going? I don't know anything about anything. I'm the beginner of all beginners. What am I expecting?"* The truth is nothing at all. I always kept secret the predictions of mystics, nor did I act upon them. I never wanted to force or influence the outcome of anything. I was simply driven to do what had to be done.

On the first of February, I departed for India, leaving behind an expecting wife, son, and parents. On the flight over, a woman approached me to ask for money. Despite thinking it odd, I conceded to the request, but what actually stuck with me was what she said.

With interest she asked, **"Why are you going to India?"**

"It's kind of a spiritual thing," I replied.

I was tempted to say, **"I really don't know,"** which was the actual truth, but out of fear of being considered demented, I chose a close approximation of it.

With an expression of experience she said, **"I thought it might be something like that, but I'll tell you something about India. It either makes you or breaks you."** At the time, I thought the second would be the most probable outcome.

After so many hours, we were finally approaching Delhi, but funny clouds covered the ground as far as the eye could see. It turned out they were not clouds but, in fact, thick layers of pollution, which is now one of the many problems that affect modern-day India. Despite the early morning hours, the airport was thriving with activity. Going through customs took quite some time, and I was dead tired. I hoped in a taxi, which looked like something out of the '50s, and tried to put on a seat belt, but the driver said, **"No, no, no, no, no, no."** (Sounded like a motor). I chuckled and thought that since the car seemed to be falling apart, strapping on a seat belt would at least give me the idea of being a little safer, but OK. The roads were mostly empty, but the driver was especially fond of honking and encroaching on other vehicles. Even on three-lane highways, he would get as close as he could to any car in sight. There are many such stories about the traffic in India, so I will not dwell on them, but strangely enough, there is a certain harmony to it, and accidents are rare.

Noida Ashram

On arrival at the YSS Noida ashram, I was already being swindled by the cab driver, which at the time I didn't take kindly but would soon get accustomed to, and in the end, despite thinking it to be wrong, I would find it to be funny. At the ashram, there seemed to be no reservation in my name. I didn't take it too seriously, but the thought of, *"What am I doing here?"* crossed my mind. Somehow, things worked out, and accommodations were arranged. That very same day, I talked with a resident swami, a lively fellow named Vinayananda. He answered my questions to the best of his ability, but I must admit, doubts in my mind still lingered, especially regarding my inability to perform techniques. Striving to ease my mind, Swami Vinayananda said something important in much the same way it was told to him: **"Look, don't worry so much, just remember that everything is a learning curve."** This is true, of course, but only if one has the right predisposition.

Although I didn't notice it right away, my suffering was gone, a welcomed relief. Realization of this came during evening service. Suddenly, meditation was easy and pleasant again. I felt refreshed. After dinner and a much-needed bath, I went to bed for the first time in three days. As soon as I laid my head and closed my eyes, I received the most passionate kiss ever. I cannot adequately explain it, it carried a certain degree of physical sensation, but it wasn't physical. I immediately stood up. "**What was this?**" I said in wonder. Despite being somewhat disconcerted by the event, I took it as an auspicious sign—a **welcome**. It was pure and beautiful.

Picture 2º - A curious "Welcome."

Life at the ashram had its own little routines, like most ashrams in India: three meals a day, morning and evening service, and regular working hours for libraries and shops, much like the scheduled sessions with Swamis and Brahmins. On Sundays, things were slightly different: A Satsang was held mid-morning, and a long three-hour service (meditation) in the evening.[10] This got me worried. I knew I could handle 90 minutes but three hours. I wanted to take part in everything, whatever it may be, so I tried to do my best and somehow survived. I encountered very good souls in the ashram: devotees, volunteers, staff, and monastics, all doing great work for the greater good. I'm sure the masters are pleased. One such person was a man named Ash. At the time, he was doing volunteer work at the library and often went out of his way to help me.

Other than strolling in the gardens, catching some sun, and practicing what I could, there wasn't much to do, so people often encouraged me to read. I never replied, but when Ash said the very same thing, I did.

"Look, I didn't come here to read. I could have done that back home. I don't know what I'm doing here... I think we are all just trying to be better men, better souls, and that should count for something in anyone's book."

My mobile didn't work in India, and I struggled to connect with my wife. On the morning of my departure, Ash was set on solving this problem. While driving to the shop, a most curious conversation took place:

Ash – **"So, do you like the Rudraksha you bought?"** [11]

Me – **"I guess. They are rare ones with certificates."**

Ash – **"I only wear this."**

---

[10] The word Satsang is made up of Sat, meaning truth, and Sang, which means together. A Satsang, therefore, is a gathering together to seek truth.

[11] Rudraksha refers to a stone fruit. These dried stones are used as prayer beads by Hindus, as well as by Buddhists and Sikhs. There are about ten kinds of Rudraksha, each with different properties, and some can be pretty expensive.

Even today, I still don´t know what it was. He was always very secretive about it, but it looked like some kind of wood necklace, a special one from what I could ascertain.

"I was going to invite you for dinner at my house to meet my family."

Me – **"Oh... but I told you I was leaving today."**

Ash – **"I must have forgotten. Are the plane fares to your country expensive?"**

Me – **"Well, that depends on the class. I recommend taking the executive class. It's a little more expensive, but it will make the trip more bearable."**

Ash – **"Is this something I can afford?"**

Me – **"Yes, I think so. I don't have a big fancy house, but you are welcome to visit. You can bring your wife if you want."**

Ash – **"Well, I was thinking about it. Are the hotels expensive? Do they have vegetarian restaurants?"**

Me – **"Look, there is no need for unnecessary expenses, you will stay in my house. I'm determined to be a vegetarian, and I think my wife will follow, so there is no reason for you to stay elsewhere."**

Ash – **"Later on, my family is going to the ashram to meet you."**

Me – **"OK... I'll finish packing up, and we can meet after lunch."**

After much trouble and difficulty, Ash managed to arrange a service provider. Unfortunately, it had no compatibility with my phone, and I would have to buy a new one, which I ended up not doing since it seemed like a waste of money. Back at the ashram, I said goodbye to everyone I could, took a bath, finished packing, and went to lunch. Soon after that, I was in the lobby waiting with my bags. Ash arrived with his son and daughter-in-law. We all respectfully greeted each other, and I took the opportunity to extend the invitation to all. As his wife approached me from behind, Ash presented me with extended hands and an expression of satisfaction. His manner of acting conveyed unspoken words.

"Look, didn't I tell you."

The wife walking sideways to her husband, looked at me with an expression of surprise and disbelief. Some words were spoken, but she took no heed and continued gazing at me in the same manner. Shortly after, I received a heartfelt embrace from Ash, and we parted ways.

All this was very strange. The wife seemed to have seen me before, although we had never met. In fact, the whole family seemed to know something I didn't. Apparently, now wasn't the time to understand the how or why, so I was kept out of the loop. I also realized that Ash was the man the mystic Templar spoke of. I didn't see him as a father, but I saw that he acted like a father figure, although the reason why still escaped me.

Ranchi

I arrived at Ranchi by the cover of night and heavy rain, so I had no idea of my surroundings. I might have been in the wrong place, but thankfully no. I was exhausted, and the hour was late. I was set on skipping practice and getting a good night's sleep. Then, consciousness knocked at my door and said: *"Stop making excuses. You'll manage."* So I sat by the edge of the bed with my feet suspended and tried my best. As it turns out, this was the best meditation I had ever experienced. *"Wow, what energy."* From that moment onward, the perception of power flowing to my center (spiritual eye) was always with me.

Morning came, and I could finally glance at my surroundings. The beautiful, jungle-like vegetation and palatial gardens came into view. What an atmosphere. Ranchi was truly a special place in more ways than one, and my awareness of this grew over time. On that very day, I met my roommate—someone who was on the same spiritual quest. We spent most of the day talking about God and His divine touch, sharing our thoughts and feelings. He was set in his mind to renounce everything—his job, family, and possessions—to wander the world, aspiring to find what can only be found within. Despite being a little worried about his extreme isolation, I understood exactly how he felt. I expressed my worry and advised him to take this opportunity and speak to one of the sannyasins. They might have some good counsel to give.[12]

I didn't want to speak to anyone myself, though. I had questions but was expecting more of the same answers, so I thought: *"What's the point."* But the very next day, I changed my mind. The cause was Swami Sudananda. A flow of energy came to me as he spoke; curiously or not, he was answering the questions that were dwelling in my mind. He was undoubtedly someone worth talking to. The next day, I met him. Though nothing of particular importance was spoken, I came to enjoy his company.

As time passed, I started to be overwhelmed with the feeling of being home. Not in a sense that Ranchi was my home or India for that matter, but a feeling of connectedness, of being closer to God. Later on, I understood that it was so. By the grace of the Guru, the veil was made thinner in this place, so even "beginners" like me could perceive the divine presence emanating from the man named Paramahansa Yogananda.

During my stay, I met an interesting devotee on pilgrimage all over India with his fiancée. He was an enthusiastic fellow, and by this time, I began to be enthusiastic too. He was going to Dakshineswar, much like I was. He started filling me in on things to see and places to go. I was all too eager to hear it. Ten days would be quite a long time to spend doing nothing. Later, he became my roommate and gave me detailed suggestions for my trip. I found myself yet again being driven and guided in what to do.

I had another curious encounter during my stay, but not with a devotee—well, not exactly. I was casually walking through the property when a young man approached me in a friendly manner. He began speaking of his life experiences, troubles, difficulties, and how he and his family were

---

[12] A sannyasin is religious ascetic who has renounced the world by performing his own funeral and abandoning all claims to social or family standing.

blessed/helped by Guru Yogananda. Yet, I was surprised to learn that he did not practice meditation. He struck me as a man of virtue and with a deep faith in Yogananda.

Me – "Really? Why not?"

The young man – "**What's the point? Many meditate and attend religious ceremonies, but it's all just for show. Inwardly, they feel differently. They act differently.**"

Me – "**I'm somewhat surprised to see such a phenomenon in India. I see Christians acting in much the same way. I guess it to be the same everywhere else.**"

The young man – "**Yes.**"

Me – "**Maybe one day you'll start meditating. You already got a leg up on most.**"

The young man – "**I don't know... maybe.**"

Shortly after, I met his father. He was of the same nature as his son, and the first thing he said to me was:

"**Do you follow the Guru's teachings?**"

I understood immediately that this was not pertaining to any meditative practice. In truth, Yogananda's teachings are the same as Jesus and any other enlightened master. There are many, I'm sure, that engage in various religious and spiritual practices to gain power and status. That's their choice, but for those who follow by ways of light-love, putting one's heart and mind in the right place can never be overly emphasized. I thought this encounter to be quite curious. Out of the ordinary, I would say. Often those I met showed only interest in knowing where I come from and little more than that. To me, this held no importance. After all, we all come from the very same place.

The moment I feared was fast approaching, the month-long service of six hours. Everyone was urging me along: "**Just do your best.**" I knew this was far beyond what I could handle, but even so, I tried. The service was being held by Swami Sudananda, and many devotees came to attend. It seems this monthly event was quite popular. I held my own until about the fifth hour, but by this time, my body was aching, and I had to move. As I did, my eyes fell upon the blissful figure of Swami Sudananda, swaying rhythmically in an ecstatic state. This made me all too aware of my own inadequacy for such things, but still, I could not give up.

It was almost time for me to move on and leave this special place behind. I gave my thanks to all and bid them farewell. By mid-afternoon, I was all but finished. Back in our room, my friend dozed off while I gazed at the view of the first-floor balcony. Suddenly, right in front of me, a great tree began to be enlivened by crows. More and more came and filled its branches from top to bottom. They would approach in turn, hovering for moments to greet me. If I had stretched out my arm, I could have touched them. The loud calls of the crows raised quite an uproar, although no one seemed to notice—not even my sleepy friend. I was very much amazed. It all seemed like a goodbye of sorts, and I was happy. I relished the moment for 30 minutes before leaving. Then, in an instant, they were gone.

At dawn the next day, my roommate and I shared a cab to the airport. To no surprise of my own, we were being swindled again. By now, I was all but used to it, but my friend didn't take it very well. I did my best to appease his distress, and we moved on.

Picture 3° - A beautiful goodbye.

My stay in Kolkata - Dakshineswar

Despite thinking at times that I might be lost, my journey to Dakshineswar was pretty much uneventful, which was a welcome novelty from what I was now accustomed to. On arrival and after being done with formalities, I was informed about a three-day event that was taking place the next day. It was basically a review of all the techniques in the lessons, but I was unsure if I wanted to take part. By now, I felt pretty comfortable with what I knew. I didn't practice the Om technique, but it looked simple enough. Kriya was the only thing that caught my eye, but I wasn't allowed to attend, so I thought: *"I'll just go to the opening ceremony and leave it at that."*

Morning came, and I wasn't expecting much, but I would nevertheless be respectful and listen attentively. As it turned out, great words of wisdom started reaching my ears, and I felt enlivened and enthusiastic. *"Who was this man? I want to hear more."* I then decided to participate in hopes of doing so. To my disappointment, Swami Achyutananda didn't preside over any of the classes I could attend. I later realized that he had already played his part by getting me to join.

Interestingly enough, the reviews being given were based on the new lessons that were due to come out very soon. I would get a first look at the improved practices well before the printed edition was in my hands. The marathon began, and I was determined to make the best of it. On the very first day, a devotee approached me and asked me to write down my notes on a particular technique. I was feeling very much unqualified and said, **"Look, aren't you better off asking one of the swamis? I think they have something planned in the schedule."**

We glanced at the schedule and saw they had 30 minutes reserved on the last day to receive all devotees. I then realized I had no choice. It would be impossible to dispel the doubts of all participants in such a short amount of time. I sighed and said, "**OK**." By the end of the event, I had all my notes transcribed in detail, which reminded me of my days back in school.

The next day a driver was arranged to take me to various spots across Kolkata. My day was filled with visits to Mother Teresa's center, Garpar Dhyana Mandir, the living quarters of the levitating saint Bhaduri Mahasaya and master Yogananda's childhood home. It is difficult for me to adequately depict the places mentioned above, especially the last one. A materialist would have little to no interest in such places, for their value lies beyond what the eye can see and the hand can touch. Only those who are receptive can perceive and understand it, but I will narrate events pertaining to two of these places.

At the Dhyana Mandir, a lesson on chanting was taking place. The man giving it was one I'd seen before in the ashram. An Indian of a stout and grave figure, straight as an arrow as far as I could tell, usually a quality not much appreciated by most. Believe me, I know. This meeting was a prelude to a later much-needed conversation, plus I got to learn a little more about chanting and its purpose.

Number 4 Garpar Road was my last stop. Yogananda's childhood home was now the living quarters of a family of devotees that, through an arrangement, became caretakers and guides of the property. This was quite a large and well-built structure; it seemed to maintain its charm from long ago. I saw all the rooms depicted in the books and even got to meditate a little in the secret attic room from his childhood. The house exuded its own particular energy, but what surprised me was a boy no more than five years old. He seemed to have the expression of the infinite in his eyes.

I said, "**This boy... This boy has something, his eyes.**"

Our hostess replied, "**The boy you see is my grandchild. I prayed to the Guru to bring me a grandson, and so he did. He bore a reddish circular mark on the kutastha (spiritual eye) at the time of his birth.**"

I then affirmed, "**Well, he definitely has something.**"

She responded with a chuckle.

After a little while, I headed back. By this time, I was determined to give all my leftover money to the ashram. So when I thought the driver was overcharging me, I wasn't very pleased. We argued a little, but he insisted. Being late and giving him the benefit of the doubt, I paid and went on my way, although very much aggrieved. I then thought this money was better off being given to the ashram than taken by unsavory characters. So I decided not to go to the home of the masters in Serampore and do just that.

The next day, I was determined, but the masters decided otherwise. For some reason, I found myself at the front desk, where I overheard a newcomer from Brazil asking to go to Serampore. I thought it to be a coincidence, but my mind kept dwelling on the subject. So I decided to approach him, and arrangements were made for us to go together and split the fare. Somehow we ended up with a party of three as an Italian devotee came to join our group.

After learning about the Om technique in detail, the thought of trying it out lingered in my mind. I thought this day was as good as any other, so after meditation, I set myself up to do so privately. A rumbling sound started to come from within me. It grew, and a strong vibration started to shake me from the core, like a subwoofer playing loudly within my chest. I experienced it for five minutes before breaking. As I finished, my hands were shaking. My whole body. "**WOW.**"

Come morning, we all agreed, as a group, to visit the Ramakrishna ashram. So we set out to catch the ferry and cross the Ganges. I got a very close look at the high level of pollution in the river, various types of waste afflicted its sacred waters, but that didn't stop many from bathing in it. Notwithstanding, the setting of the red sun over the Ganges was always a breathtaking sight. We docked, and after a very short walk, we were at the doors of the Ramakrishna ashram. What a huge complex with multiple temples, structures, and an impressive museum. Our Brazilian friend was trying to capture it all on camera, but no such desire awoke within me. I wanted to take something back, yes, but within my heart, within my soul.

Something quite curious happened here, although I am yet to understand it. As we were approaching a courtyard teeming with people, a solitary sannyasin waved me to come and sit by his side. He had a short white boxed beard and unusual rainbow eyes, even more so for an Indian. This man sitting by a young tree seemed to be apart from everything else. I agreeably sat down beside him. He then began speaking in Bengali, or so I thought. I could only tell what appeared to be the number four at the end.

He said, "**Something, something, something <u>four</u>... something.**"

He would show me four fingers and then point to the sky. He said it three or four times, always expressing himself with his hand.

I replied, "**I don't understand. I don't understand.**"

This was all I could say. At the time, I thought the sannyasin was asking for money, which was total nonsense. That solitary man was trying to convey something important, yet I failed to grasp it. Could I have done something differently? Something better?

I said goodbye affectionately and rejoined my group, but that man's gaze was never far from me. By morning's end, we headed back to the ashram and, to our satisfaction, just in time for lunch. After that, we were driven to Serampore, home of Sri Yukteswar and master Yogananda, for many years. What an atmosphere. The other side of the Ganges felt like another world. The light was different, the air, the energy, I cannot explain it better. Upon visiting the land that saw the holy feet of the masters, I felt blessed. A joy filled my heart and mind.

We continued our journey, which led back to places I'd already been, but I didn't mind. Our last stop was Nº 4 Garpar Road, and by rule, the devotees were only allowed to visit the home of the Guru once. As such, I ended up waiting in the entrance hall for the others. I was so tired that I sat down and closed my eyes. Such peace filled me. *"How come? Even here, such energy."* I was surprised but enjoyed every moment of it. An hour later, we left and got some much-needed sleep that night.

During my stay, I refrained from giving charity to anyone, least of all money, but I wanted to present an offering to someone I passed by almost every day. As far as I could tell, he was a homeless, elderly man of delicate constitution. He would sit every day in the building facing the ashram where I was staying. He was apparently doing nothing, just quietly watching. I would pass by him often and began offering some pieces of fruit or the prasad I was given. He always accepted, although somewhat reluctantly.[13]

---

[13] Prasad is a devotional offering made to a deity, typically consisting of food that is later shared among devotees.

I knew that my gestures were of little importance or significance, but I didn't want to leave without presenting him with an offering of various fruits. One morning right after breakfast, I got an opportunity to do just that. I approached him and imparted my gift, which he took with surprise. I bowed respectfully and left, but he called me back and started speaking in Bengali. I didn't understand a word and thought to myself: *"Great, this again."* I kept saying, **"Sorry, I don't understand. Sorry, I don't understand. I don't understand."**

Finally, I bowed and turned to leave, but the man promptly yelled, calling me back. As he began speaking, something wondrous happened. I can only describe it as a scene from a sci-fi movie. Like when you're watching beings of an alien race speaking to each other in a language of their own, and all of a sudden, segments of conversation began to get translated into something you can understand. I began listening with rapt attention.

"... **I never take money**... **God and Guru say that money is impure**...

"**Normally, I don't accept food from others, for it is tainted by wrong intent.**"

When he said this, I felt that he accepted what I was giving and said, "**It comes from the heart.**"

We bowed in turn to each other and parted ways. This reference to money stuck with me, but in time I also realized that things were not always that simple, and at times exceptions could be made to render righteous aid to those in need.

Devotees, usually way more advanced than I, would often approach me and state that they finally found what they were seeking. Some after searching for many, many years. I was always happy to hear it but was unsure about my ability to get there. One day during the afternoon tea, my Italian friend and I were alone in the cafeteria, which was quite unusual. Sharing the moment, a conversation ensued. He started making a lively account of the techniques, his experience, and his journey. He was a really nice fellow, and his disclosure uplifted my spirit. Quite an enjoyable moment over a wonderful cup of tea (Chai).

It was almost time to put an end to my stay in India, but not without enduring another six-hour-long service. I barely "survived" the previous. Still, I was willing to try. We were all set to begin the energization exercises, as we always do before meditation. Evenly spread out and ready to start, I was focused, eyes closed, calmly waiting for the signal to begin. Suddenly a wave of energy struck me from behind, throwing me five feet forward, almost over the chairs in front of me. The others gazed at me inquisitively as I tried to stop, as though breaking from a sprint. Puzzled and trying not to draw too much attention, I stepped back into position.

Picture 4° - Struck by a wave of energy.

This was not the work of any person, for no one stood behind me, nor was it the wind. Nothing else was thrown out of position, not even the plastic chairs in front of me. All I can say is this was something unique. A wave of energy is the best I can describe it.

The service began, and by the fourth hour, I started to struggle. With great difficulty, I managed to hold on until the end. I looked like a zombie, utterly drained of life force. I was eager to sleep and rest, but not without grabbing a little something to eat.

The following day I said my definite goodbyes to all and got to speak for a while with the stout Indian I had met earlier. I wanted to ask some questions and follow the rituals in the ashrams.

Me – "I was so drained from yesterday that I didn't feel like talking. I want to do all these things and more, but I seem to lack the ability for them. This is all so difficult for me. I'm not gonna give up. I'm not a quitter."

Man – "You're doing too much. Many beginners are like that. Just strive to meditate morning and evening. If you stay longer, that's fine. If not, that's OK too. Just don't push so much."

Me – "I always think I do too little, not enough, or good enough."

"Should I use incense in my practice?"

Man – "Some people don't do well with it. I use scented candles. It's like a two-in-one."

Me – "How should I chant? For how long?"

Man – "Chant or don't chant. Do it if it helps. We usually chant for five to seven minutes. For more extended periods (3 to 6h), we chant for ten to fifteen minutes every hour. You can chant these songs or others."

Me – "I want to be a vegetarian, and the Indian way seems like the right way to do it. Is there somewhere I can learn?"

Man – "**Sure, there are plenty of books and YouTube tutorials you can check out.**"[14]

I embraced and thanked him. After that, I caught a cab to start a very long ride home. I was hoping to wave goodbye to that homeless man, but somehow our eyes never met. By this time, my bags were full of accessories and other paraphernalia that I did and didn't need, things I thought might help me on the road to travel. Later, I would come to think differently.

---

[14] This turned out to be no more than wishful thinking. No matter my efforts, things just taste different in India.

Chapter Eight

Home Again

The journey back was long and tiresome, but my wife and son were happy to see me back. On the very next day, I enrolled for the new SRF lessons and hoped to receive them on time. With the previous version, I often stayed more than a month with no material, which always left me anxious. To no surprise, all my ordeals were back. Everything was extremely difficult again. Despite this being true, my dreams were different, and the flow of energy going through the spiritual eye never left me. This force, at times, struck me like a bullet through the brain, and other times it felt like a piercing needle. Later on, it appeared to be frying my center. I could hear it, and feel it. Over time it evolved in quality, quantity, and consistency. Soon I began to understand and have realizations/perceptions that I believed not to be my own. I struggled for a long time, avoiding writing about them, but a higher authority eventually drove me to it, and I will share them all in due time.

The afflictions of the mind disturbed me greatly. These distorted thoughts would often attack my mind, causing distress, and the more I tried not to think about them, the more I did. What ended up helping me was a psychological tool: a phrase with no meaning or sense to it that broke the line of thought. Speed and repetition were the keys to dissolving these thoughts. One just needs to properly recognize them. This temporary tool helps until such time as we become less receptive to these forms of attack.

Sleep

I never gave much importance to sleep. *"It's just a thing we do."* I thought. Now that I slept almost nothing at all, I perceive things differently and understand so much more. I could say the exact same thing about dreams. I rarely dreamed and paid no heed to them when I did, they would usually fade away as quickly as they came, but now they were different in so many ways. It's true that one should not live in a world of dreams, but dreams can become spiritual tools for learning and healing.

The great sages of old say that the soul that dwells in minerals sleeps, that it dreams in plants, awakens in animals, and knows it is awake in man, with his sense of I. As the soul goes forward in its own process of evolution, it grows increasingly aware of the seeming reality of the physical world. The pure divine nature of the soul is ill-suited for this world, so the Infinite Intelligence devised a way to stabilize all forms in existence for the benefit of the "soul" and its creation.

Every life form in creation sleeps, whatever it may be. Some forms of life are said not to sleep and yet have states of being very similar to sleep. At times, the phenomena may appear absent due to the simplicity of the organism, its short life span, and/or its frenetic activity. Still, these often have states of suspended animation, where they remain "dormant" until conditions are suitable for them to express "life."

No being can live without or resist this divinely ordained state of sleep. Those who resist it provoke great harm to themselves but ultimately cave to this higher force. Some are indeed afflicted with sleeping disorders, but they are caused by the actions of those who have them. The worst of them is Fatal Familial Insomnia (FFI), which, over time and much suffering, leads to death.

So, what is sleep? We can go into the technical definition of it, but what's important here is to differentiate between sleep with dreams and dreamless sleep, which is a higher, purer form of sleep. We usually dream in our sleep, even if we're unaware of it. This is the regular sleeping pattern in contrast to dreamless sleep, which is rare. The construct of dreams requires a significant amount of energy which impairs the full recovery of body and mind. Dreamless sleep has no such obstruction which allows the "free" flow of the divine within ourselves. Each one of us, at one time or another, has experienced this deep form of sleep. It usually comes in short bursts leaving one with a sense of joy, energy, and relaxation.

In sleep, you connect with the force that gives and sustains life, so the body and mind are replenished to go on living. Bearing weight in this process is the condition of everyone's instrument, but the best most of us can expect is just to be a little more rested. Content on being able to go on with our daily lives, often enough with a shot of caffeine. Of course, this need not be the case, and room for improvement is always at hand, but not without some effort.

Dreams and Visions

It may seem that I'm vilifying dreams, but that's not my intent. Dreams can be important, and they do serve a purpose. Spiritual dreams are tools of the divine that help us perceive what we cannot in "waking" life. As such, they should not be dismissed. Some dreams are clearer and easier to understand, while others not so much, and their meaning comes only later in life. Whichever the case may be, they both remain imprinted in memory. These dreams express themselves as part of a movie on display, where the temporal factor might be key or it may not. You can be part of this movie in a myriad of different ways, or you may not. The dreamer is usually not consciously active in dreams. He only takes what is given.

As I mentioned earlier, we often dream in our sleep. Dreams you can't remember, or that fade from memory are unimportant. The exception to this would be vivid dreamers. They "live" and remember dreams, even if they are devoid of significant content and/or value. However, these souls have the potential for so much more, and striving to gain conscious awareness in dreams is critical in that process.

Spiritual dreams are indeed special. They have a different feel to them, which can only be understood through experience. Very few are born with the gift of having an open channel through sleep. Fewer still are those who can teach how to hone and develop this gift. Notwithstanding, if you are born with the gift of true dreams, you would be doing a disservice to the One who gave it if you were to ignore it.

Visions can also be of different types, but they differ from dreams. There is a conscious, interactive factor to a higher or lesser degree. Visions also have a particular framing, and the self can easily identify its origin as coming from one's center, the spiritual eye. I would like to finish on this subject by saying: There are dreams of a negative/dark influence, just like in waking life. In this world, we are subject to all things positive and negative, but in time you will come to see all things in a positive way.

A Glimpse of Past Lives

After a while, I began to see glimpses of past lives, although, at the time, I didn't fully believe or understand. These were given in two separate moments and shown in different ways.

The first was given in a dream of a very vivid nature. Even though I didn't like it, I never forgot it. I was fleeing with a woman through what appeared to be catacombs made of large stone. At a certain point, we found ourselves trapped, almost waist-deep in water. Escape was out of reach just beyond a high-up barred window. An animus figure approached us. A bare-chested man, bald, well built, of grey complexion and pitch-black sclera. Dark veins seemed to protrude from his head and body. We backed up from his presence as far as we could, until we could no more. A blaze of darkness shot out from his extended hand and struck her. I grabbed hold as her life was consumed by a pale grey decay. With her last breath, a curse was cast. It took the form of a blot that merged onto the back of the animus figure. She then died in my arms as he departed with complete disregard for my presence. Strangely enough, I felt no animosity toward this man. I didn't want to hurt him, nor did I want him to hurt us.

Shortly after, a little more disclosure was given to this story. There's no timeline, but our setting was Egypt. Whereas an infant, I was taken by the leader of a dark cult who ritualistically murdered my family. I was then raised in the black arts and continued in ignorance until the decision to break from this madness. Half of the cult members left with me. Needless to say, this wasn't well received by my father figure, who, in the end, killed me with a dagger through the heart. I can tell you that this was no random event. I was purposefully targeted, taken at a very young age to be molded. Used to hold power, manipulate, enslave, and oppress others.[15]

My second glimpse into the past was of a brighter nature. A dream revealed that I lived as a Yogi in two previous incarnations. First, I was a renunciant of dark complexion and matted hair, a vagrant in the world. In a second life, I seemed to be a swami—a thin, tall man of whitish complexion. I saw this in the form of two pictures. One was a shoot in front of an ashram where I stood with my brothers. On another, I stood alone, with large horned cows in the background. I perceived the latter life experience to have been of greater service and purpose. I needed to see and know these things but still struggled to consider myself worthy.

As days went by, my struggle continued. I longed to know more. *"What am I to do? How am I to do it?"* I then thought of asking my sister Sara for a psychic reading. I already had one many years ago (2011), but I must admit that I wasn't paying much attention. In fact, the only thing I can remember was a word - Chidananda. This word came suddenly and completely out of context as she spoke. We both acted in surprise.

I asked, **"What is this? What does it mean?"**

Nothing came, just a word with no connection to anything before or after. Upon starting in the spiritual life, I thought this might become my name. I later realized this was the name of the current President of the Self-Reali-

---

[15] It's curious to use the expression "random event" because in a sense nothing in creation is truly random, although it may look like it to many of us.

zation Fellowship. Trying to make sense of it all, I thought another session with my sister might clarify things. Point me in the right direction. So, arrangements were made a month from now to do just that.

Chapter Nine

Close Revelations

A few days after the arrangement, I left home to go for a stroll. I remember that right upon leaving, invisible tears started running down my cheeks, like channels branching out from a mainstream. I could feel the wind brushing against them but could not touch or see them. This went on for almost an hour. I was puzzled. I wasn't sad or anything: *"Why? What does this mean?"* I tried researching this phenomenon but could find no reference to it. Later on, the answer would be given in much the same way as it was given to me. This is the first time I have spoken/written about it, like many other things portrayed in this book. I'm usually very secretive about such things, especially when I have little to no understanding of them, but I will come to share as much as I can.

My wife was almost a month away from delivery, and since our first child was born by way of C-section, she started expressing the desire to have a natural birth. I said, **"Sure, if that's what you want. Pray for it."**

Shortly after, an answer to her expressed desire came to me in a dream. From what I could tell, we were in some kind of a hospital in the astral world. My wife was lying in bed, and a woman was assessing her condition but not in a conventional way. She then addressed me thus:

"This has nothing to do with meditation or any spiritual practice."

I immediately understood that this was due to her body. For whatever reason, it was impossible for the baby to be delivered naturally. Upon awakening, I told her as much, but she didn't seem all that convinced and said that she nevertheless had to do her part. I replied, "**Of course**."

Picture 5° - A metaphysical sadness.

A month passed, and my sister arrived from abroad. Soon after, we arranged for a night session, making sure not to be disturbed by anyone. The following is a complete and detailed depiction of our session. No parts were omitted, for everything seemed important and relevant.

After a period of concentration, we began:

"Sara" (Breathing heavily) – "I'm feeling energy, WOW... an extremely powerful one. I have never felt anything like it."

"It's approaching me from the side. It's coming from you, but it's not yours. No, it is yours but not yours at the same time. This experience is new. This goes beyond psychic readings."

"I see a figure sitting in a chair just like I am. I don't know if it's one of your spiritual masters or who it might be."

"You should communicate with this presence without words. Let it take hold of you, merge with you, and speak through you."

She then reported that this presence was forcing her to say the following. As she did, she began to cry heavily.

"What's stopping you... just trying to say it makes me feel such sadness, but this sadness is not my own."

"You feel you don't deserve this. That you're unworthy of it."

I started crying also.

Me – "Who am I? That is what I think. Who am I...?"

"Sara" – "But you don't understand that what you feel is not true. That unworthiness you feel, that depth of humility, only diminishes you and me."

"How can I explain this. This divinity is connected to you. You are one. The realization will come when you recognize you are of the same essence, which is unchangeable. There is no need to do anything to deserve that grace."

The crying continued.

"I don't know who this entity is, but you have a connection with this being, although I cannot say who it is. The image that comes to me is of a blueish figure, much like the one you have in your book."

This book, "*God talks to Arjuna*" by Sri Paramahansa Yogananda, was resting on a table next to the couch, and my sister caught a glimpse of it before sitting down.

Me – "What... Krishna?"

"Sara" – "**You have to connect with this entity through the heart. What's preventing you is you. Your need to understand. Your feelings of unworthiness.**"

"Your objective is not far from you. It's not years away. You can reach it almost instantly if you understand that this human perception of divinity is blocking you. That expression of divinity you had is but a tiny glimpse of what is."

"Your windows of liberation (meditation) are just that, windows to free you from human delusion. The spark that dwells in you is of the same essence as the divine, who placed it within you to manifest in human form, but at the same time, you have your own personality. I don't know if this makes any sense."

Me – "Yes, it does."

"Sara" – "To achieve this goal, you have to deconstruct these thoughts of yours and see that you are already divine in nature. Why do you think you need all these steps? You need no steps. Your mind makes you think in this way out of a sense of service, to become worthy of it, but you already are."

"You need to know that no one is asking you to do this, to do things in this way. The process of illumination might happen, and it most certainly does, in a singular fashion for each individual."

"There is no time to waste, for you have a job, a mission to awaken the consciousness of men. There is no time to lose. This is a critical moment, a turning point but on a global scale. Where things can go very well or very wrong. It's a conscious choice that you will give to thousands of people."

"I know you are asking how this will come to be."

Me – "**Yes.**"

"Sara" – "**You don't have to worry about that. Things will happen when and in the way they need to happen.**"

"**Remember your process doesn't have to last decades, for you are One. In your practice, work with the presence. Invite it. The timings, the chanting, the sequence, the techniques, and the prayers can help, but for you, they might work more as a distraction. You worry too much about the execution, the technique, and the order. The more you do so, the more you are diverted from its mastery.**

You should practice, of course, but you are not the one that should be doing it. You are not the doer of anything. Let that presence take you and guide you."

<u>PAUSE</u>

Now let's pause here for a moment, for this is essential. I have definitely been guilty of this. I would usually fail to be in the moment. The focus on the process often led me to brush off spiritual experience.

<u>CONTINUE</u>

"**The way to do this is to really trust what you do. You require confirmation and validation, and it's OK at first, but they can become shackles like the ones you have on your feet.**"

"**You definitely needed a Guru, but you didn't need to go to India, for you had already found him. You didn't need to go there, but you had to go there. Summon this presence to teach you firsthand. Surrender to it.**"

"**For you, the techniques are secondary. Do you know why?**"

Me – "**No.**"

"Sara" – "**The techniques are only important for those who need the steps to reach heaven. You just have to allow heaven to come to you. If you are trying to summon the presence for one hour or two and nothing comes, don't waste your time on techniques.**"

"I want you to understand that enlightenment is at your fingertips. I know this is too much for you to comprehend or accept. Well, you can understand it. You just can't accept it. Because all the other gurus did it differently, why should you be different? Shouldn't you go through the same process? Shouldn't you go through an even more complicated process because you are so much worse than them?"

Me – "Yep, that is right."

"Sara" – "You must understand that these are different times. There is an entirely different human collective consciousness from what was thousands of years ago or even a hundred years ago."

"It is very difficult for the western world to grasp things the way India conveys them, and that's your job. It's all about language, all about presence."

"I'm not sure what I'm seeing, but I will try to describe it. I see some sort of cone on your head, with little balls protruding from it, and it appears to be turning on itself. You have many arms, four arms on each side, and as they move, music of a repetitive nature echoes in the background."

She didn't understand it, nor did I at the time.

"I don't know what this is, but bodhisattva comes to mind."

"Let illumination come in a passive way that at the same time is active. Past, present, and future are the eternal now, which is the key to your enlightenment."

"Let go of your mind, be receptive without thinking. Don't expect anything, and maybe something wondrous will happen."

"I was expecting this session to go in a certain way, and that created resistance."

Me – "I was expecting something different too."

"Sara" – "This focus on the process creates difficulties, don't mistake the technique for the goal. Words have power, no doubt, but they are secondary to experience. You have a live Guru within yourself, don't deny your experience."

Me – "I do?"

"Sara" – "Yes, that bluish figure. If something feels right or wrong, why do you ignore it?"

Me – "I want to follow the guidance of the masters, but now that you put it like that."

"Sara" – "Your question from earlier, I heard it, and I'm going to give you the answer."

My question was: *"Why things had to happen in this way?"*

"You know your body very well. What did you do when you ate something that didn't feel right?"

Me – "I didn't eat it. Something might be off, the timing, quantity, or the product itself."

"Sara" – "Just try to do your thing. You have a massive resistance to your wisdom. You usually say to yourself, '*What the hell do I know.*' "

Me – "Yep, that is correct."

"Sara" – "When I say you should summon this entity, I'm not saying call it from a million light-years away. I'm saying ignite the spark. Let the divine take the rains, trust. Trust lives in not knowing. Trust lives in the darkness."

"You have to adapt the techniques to you. You have developed a very keen sense of knowing what is right and wrong, a highly developed judgment. You don't need permission, but this is certainly not true for everyone."

"Think. Why did these things happen to you if you're unworthy? They were meant to happen, for the divine has found you worthy. You were chosen."

"Your job is to awaken the consciousness of man, but each individual has his own choice to make, to change or not to change. Your presence goes beyond words, and it calls to others. It sparks something within them, but it's not your job to maintain it. They can follow you if they want, but that's not your part."

"You know what these spiritual experiences feel like. You've had a glimpse of the real deal, no matter how long or short they were, so now you can recognize when you are experiencing the real thing."

This was a really long and intense session. I couldn't really understand it: *"Was I possessed or something? Were there two souls within me?"* It was like I was listening but not ready to listen. Despite knowing the "**Bhagavad Gita**," I didn't really understand the figure of Krishna. I knew in my heart it was very important; I just didn't know how or why. Only now, as I am writing this, do I realize the truth and the connection to these events.

Upon writing this, a dream came to me. At first, I didn't give it much thought, but suddenly I understood. I was a graduate, certificate in hand, when suddenly I felt the urge to pursue a degree in something else. In a split second, I found myself in school again, if I'm not mistaken, the seventh grade. I didn't much care for it. It seemed to be a waste of my time, like I didn't belong. Shortly after, a friendly figure approached and sat by my side.

He said, "**You don't need to stay in the seventh grade.**"

I exclaimed in surprise, "**Really! Can I go to the tenth grade?**"

Gazing at me with compassion he replied, "**Why would you want to go to the tenth grade. Why not be a finalist? Why not do only one subject?**"

I realized that I had traveled this road before—that I was just this close to achieving what I wanted, and there was no need to go through it all again. I just couldn't realize it at the time.

My wife's pregnancy was coming to a close, although her body said otherwise, as the unripe cervix hinted that labor was likely to be induced.

This news didn't upset my wife all that much. She just didn't want another C-section. At our last medical appointment, the doctor said in a very lively manner, "**This is looking good. It's all up to you.**" Now, this got my wife really pumped up. She started squatting, running, cleaning, and don't get me wrong, it's nice to see things all spic and span, but I didn't want her to get her hopes up.

I said, "**Look, I know you're happy, but remember what we've been told.**"

"**I know, I'm just doing my part,**" she replied with confidence.

The scheduled day for delivery arrived, and the doctors said—no surprise to me—that the cervix was far from ripe and labor would have to be induced. She would have to be admitted and stay overnight under surveillance. As such, I decided to depart, spend the night at home, and hopefully return in the morning. By midnight, the baby started showing signs of distress, and a C-section had to be performed, much like last time. The baby, still afflicted by drugs, had to stay under observation for a few days, but everything turned out alright.

A few days later, I had an intriguing dream. I saw glimpses of a horse running free, and at the same time, a passage—like in scripture—kept appearing repeatedly. It read thus. "*Enjoy the deaded debtor.*"

I almost immediately woke up in surprise. *"How was this possible? How could I have no more Karmic debt?"* Since I started my learning process, in the back of my mind, I had always wondered how much bad karma I had stored from previous lives. This was surely something I needed to know, although I didn't fully believe it yet.

The Life and Spiritual Journey of No One

Chapter Ten

"Sin"

The concept of "sin" was always very much alive in my mind. Thoughts about deeming a variety of things as 'sin' were a constant. I strongly advise devotees to avoid this mistake. The more you dwell on these thoughts, the more you soil your mind. You'll find yourself more focused on what keeps you from Him than on what gets you closer to Him, and this is a fault prevalent in many religions. So I started wondering: *"Where does "sin" come from?"* Some say that Adam and Eve were the original cause. The ones who committed the original "sin" that gave birth to all "sins," drowning themselves and countless generations in darkness and ignorance. The "sinful" act of eating the apple symbolizes engagement in physical intimacy to some and the acquisition of knowledge to others. Whichever the case, it seems convenient to blame all the miseries of this world on Adam and Eve.

The story of Adam and Eve is indeed a curious one. So, God gave sexual organs to Adam and Eve, but at the same time forbade them from touching or using them. This seems to be quite contradictory. It's like giving you eyesight and then telling you not to see. On the other hand, this perception of the story goes against one of God's most critical Universal Laws—Free Will. The same thing could be said about the intellect in men. The pursuit of knowledge is not wrong in itself. Quite the opposite, mankind should always strive to better itself. The issue may come from the act of giving knowledge prematurely. The self-aware being is not always prepared to receive certain grades of knowledge. If the time's not right, knowledge can do more harm than good.

We do tend to blame others for our pain and sorrow, but know that everything is as it should be. Some say that sexual intercourse was brought about to create offspring, but this is not the gist of it, only a part of it. The sexual energy and the reproductive organs in man do not serve one purpose only but many. The most important one is that it allows us to experience varied forms of interpersonal interactions.

In the Universal process of evolution, God comes to experience through different grades of life, but in the self-aware entity, things are different. Here, the "true" range of experience comes into play, and physical intimacy is just one of its expressions. The act can be a powerful and beautiful experience of connection to another if done in the right state of mind. In effect, this bonding is an opportunity to experience, express, and nurture love and compassion for one another. It allows us to see unity in some way or form. We are all brothers and sisters, sons and daughters of someone, parents, grandparents, etc. Still, we fail to see unity in its basic forms and consider our family nucleus to be different and more important than others.[16]

There is an essential point behind all this, and that is to see how in religion, teaching and guiding are sometimes done through negative means. "Sin" is, of course, the more obvious form, but there are others, and at times they may take very subtle forms, making them very hard to detect. Don't you find this curious? Don't these forms of teaching, more often than not, generate fear and discord? Don't they tip the scale even further towards the ways of judgment and less towards the ways of love and understanding? Doesn't this strike you as curious?

One other such example is the prophecies of doom. A common feature of many religions that mainly serves to strike fear in the hearts of men. But those who act under the influence of fear, forgetting to be wise, loving, and compassionate, are bound to bring about that which they aim to prevent.

---

[16] Be mindful that this, shall we call it, gimmick of the sexes is not in play in all corners of the Universe. There are places where things are not in this way, and in such places, these things are not wanted or needed, and this might be due to more than one reason.

God is pure Love and Wisdom, should not love and wisdom suffice in bringing us closer to Him, in opposition to fear and judgment. I ask you to introspect and See: What do you feel when faced with forms of expression made through the positive? What do you feel when they are made through the negative? I believe the answer will become quite clear.

The Life and Spiritual Journey of No One

Chapter Eleven

The Path

In time all souls are called upon to journey back to the Creator. They usually become weary, tired of this life, of this world. So they begin to seek something, although most of the time, they know not what they seek. At times this starts at a very young age. In some, a traumatic event makes them rethink life; in others, God calls upon them in a certain way and time. No two story are the same. The road of lifetimes is many, as many are the ways of the Lord our Father.

At a certain point, the seeker discovers that the something they are searching for is God. Then he sets out on a quest to reach Him and find Him. God always aids the true seeker, pointing the way to follow, guiding them home. In all true scriptures, in a more or less explicit manner, there are descriptions of practices, observances, and rules of conduct given by the divine servants of the One to aid His children.

But the truth is that you can do little to nothing at all. I'm not saying that these things aren't important. They are. I say this in the sense that you are not the doer. All these guidelines are given to put oneself in the right state of being (body, mind, and spirit). One should understand, as one often does, that this giving is less than perfect, but perfection is not required. Realize that the forces of love and light work with you, nudging you toward the goal. It's funny to see ourselves pushing to elevate our souls, trying to do so much when we can do so little.

Only God can elevate the soul in the time and manner He sees fit, primarily in accordance with the entity's ability to withstand the process. We must also consider personal karma, inherited karma (Country, Religion), desires, habits, tendencies, and more. This is no simple matter. We all struggle, but some are bound to struggle more than others. For those in the West, Saint John of the Cross makes a very accurate account of the process in the book **"Dark Night of the Soul."** Still, no matter how precise a written or spoken exposition may be, it will always dim in comparison to the reality of the one who lives it. Even so, I could never turn away from it.

This is not the way for all. For those who inherit the spirituality of India, the process is different. Focus is set on Love and Wisdom, while pain, "sin," and evil appear to be more of a side note. Many practices and observances that are to be performed in the spiritual life, to a greater or lesser degree, are commonplace in the Indian tradition/religion. Not to speak of the divine energy emanating from this land. This is not to say that it is easy. It may be easier, but a certain amount of effort is required. Whatever your case may be, never give up. The One never gives up on you.

Pain and My Personal Dark Night of the Soul

My ordeals haven't subsided even one bit. A great heaviness still lingered over me. Pain, stiffness, and distress of various kinds still pervaded my days, but some were harder than others.

Many state that pain is an illusion, which is true but not particularly helpful. Pain is all too real to the one who feels it, be it spiritual, mental, or physical. Try to refrain from making such remarks to those who live it, for such words will only mock the suffering of others. Realize also that pain is not without its purpose. No matter how unpleasant, pain is and always will be a precursor for change and growth.

For those who find themselves in such plights, I want to say that you are loved more than anything. All the pains felt and inflicted echo throughout the Universe. No cry goes unheard. No plea goes unanswered. Remember that no one is forgotten, no one. With this in mind, endure and accept the things you cannot change, and try your utmost to change the things you can.

I always thought that real love was not of this world. It was more like a word to be thrown around without any pure meaning or feeling. Even the closest relationships were conditional in nature. Very few were exceptions. This fact only increased my feeling of not belonging, of not fitting in. Despite being an athletic, smart, good-looking kid, I never really fit in. Nothing made any sense. Growing up, I made several attempts to belong but failed miserably, not just because I didn't accomplish the objective but because I felt miserable for even trying.

I feel the most intense misery, it comes in waves, sometimes high and at other times low, but it's always there. I live consciously in limbo. Constantly grasping for air where there's none to be had. I do not regret the knowledge I've gained (never). Ignorance is poison for the wise and unwise alike. At the very least, now I have a chance to accomplish what I wanted. Sometimes I feel helpless and useless, no good as a father, husband, son, or friend. I might as well be dead. In fact, I welcome death.

These pains of separation were terribly sharp and dreadful, but do not worry if such things afflict you. They do not last forever. I can now see that these mental/physical pains are, in part, caused by the seeker themselves. The root cause of this is the overwhelming eagerness felt by the devotee, who in turn strives to force the Divine connection with total disregard for the ability of the mind and body to follow. You have to work with the instruments you've been given. Mind, body, and spirit must harmonize to establish, hold, and deepen your connection with the One Infinite Intelligence. There is no other way. Had these words been given to me during my ordeals, I might have understood their truth, but I would still see myself forcing my way through for quite some time before this truth finally dawned on me.

Religion - The Guiding Hand of "God"

In different times and places around the world, God, through a chosen few (saints, prophets, special souls), has touched the lives of many. The core truths given through these souls are the same, but they are conveyed in a way and form best suited to that particular age and people. Not only that, these teachings foresee how that religion will grow and touch others over time. It's curious to see how we tend to claim ownership over the divine omnipresent. Truth doesn't belong to any one person or group. It belongs to all. It's not bound by concepts of time and space, it's not created, it doesn't change or disappear, nor does it depend on location. Truth is eternal, everywhere. You have but to find it within yourself.

We are so focused on our differences that we cannot see their underlying unity. The core truths given in most religions can, if taken in the right spirit, strengthen communities, develop societies, and breed harmony and peace, but things seem to take a wrong turn at one point or another. One might even argue that so much blood has been spilled in the name of God and religion that it would be best to live without them. This, of course, is not true. There will always be those who misuse the name of God and His teachings to harm themselves and others. But if humanity were left to fend for itself, how much more steeped in ignorance would it be? How much more would people sink into darkness or, worse, remain stuck in the middle?

The tale of Noah, from the book of Genesis, is a testimony to this truth. Contrary to popular belief, the partial dissolution of the Earth was not an act of anger. The root cause of the flood was an infringement on Universal Law that would ultimately lead to the fall of the self-aware into darkness, with no possibility of escape. As such, correction was needed. Afterward, the world might fall yet again into darkness, but it would do so of its own accord. For a time, I thought that with today's technology, maybe things would be different. Later on, the divine gave me the answer in the most epic, vivid dream I ever had.

I was looking out the attic window of my parent's house, but I didn't see the city where I lived. The first thing I noticed was massive dark clouds in the sky. They were in a circular motion with a gigantic dark hole in the middle, from which a tornado started to form. I looked down towards the land, but to my surprise, there was little land to be found. Most of it was submerged by water, with just a few mountain peaks and scattered sky-scrapers showing their faces.[17]

I realized that these buildings/structures were no bigger than pebbles, as if I was watching the scene from very high in the sky (I estimate 26,000 feet or 8,000 meters). At this point, I noticed something in the background. A massive wall of water, a wave of epic proportions that no words can describe. It stretched out far beyond what the eye could see, and though I was high in the sky, the wave extended way above me, like it could touch the stratosphere. The wave would soon engulf me as it would everything else. I crouched as it was about to hit me (as if this could help). At this point, my attention was turned to a water vortex forming on the wall next to me. I was wonderstruck as the vortex continued to expand. I asked myself, "**What is this?**"

As soon as I did, I was transported to a beach unlike any I'd seen before. The weather was calm, sunny, and warm, with a mild wind. I gazed at the vast body of water. Surprisingly, its waters were still, and only mild ripples hit the shore. I was filled with a sense of peace. At that moment, a figure appeared. His head and features were that of a bird, and his body was human-like. I had no idea who this figure was, but it seemed familiar somehow. He started speaking, but I could hardly tell or remember what he said. Only this comes to mind:

"Don't stress, do what you can, what you must."

As the figure walked away, something caught my attention. The sight of dead people half-buried in the sand, with their arms and heads sticking out.

---

[17] I call these structures sky-scrapers in order to give an idea of their size, but they bore no similarity to the structures we see today in our world.

They were frozen with their eyes and mouths open, screaming in fear and pain. A testimony to their suffering in death. Their skin appeared glazed as tears and saliva shone in the sun. Some seemed to be there for longer than others, as discoloration in the teeth and inner skin (throat and tongue) could attest. In my mind, I wondered:

"What happened? How could this be? How could these people be frozen solid in such a warm place?"

Strangely enough, I never felt fear in this whole experience.

The sight I was given was not of this Earth. It was the answer to a particular query in my mind. The purpose of the flood was not to annihilate but to reset humanity. None would live that were not meant to do so. Noah's case was indeed special—one of divine conception and purpose. However, there were other "arks" of sorts, other seeds of life scattered around the world. Those who survived were indeed few in number, but they served their purpose, as did the flood. So, one should not think that this and that religion are "wrong." They all play a part in the process of each soul. You will come to travel through many roads. Do so with open hearts and minds. You will see that they will ultimately merge into One.

Chapter Twelve

The Journey Continues - Life & Practice

One can say that I was nothing but consistent, although I saw no consistency in my practice. I say this in the sense that my spiritual practice was terrible, and within the scale of terrible, it was full of ups and downs. Even the Om technique that I was so eager to begin turned out to be a disappointment and a challenge. *"Where was that experience I had when I first tried it in India?"* As I battled with the inner obstacles, I had to tackle the outer ones too. During my windows of practice, there was little to no silence. Most of the time, it was like a Zoo out there. In fact, I would probably have found more peace and quiet at the Zoo. I joke a little, but I believe some of you can relate to my feelings. I tried many times to explain the importance of what I was doing and that some respect was necessary, but to no avail. Only when I started practicing at 5 a.m. did I begin finding some silence, but for some reason, practice always seemed more effective in the evenings.

My son, as I said earlier, was quite a hand full. Of all things, he now began assaulting school teachers and staff. I often thought: *"How could someone so gifted be afflicted by so many things?"* I know this is of his own doing, and before I tell you the following story, let me give you some context.

My wife and I are quiet, peaceful people. We uphold moral values, rules of conduct, and education. Since a very young age, we've raised our son by these core values and principles, nurturing his body and mind, but he was always a troubled child. Hyperactive, prone to bouts of negativity and highs of excitement, moods, and anger rule his life, making him easy prey to ignorance. Everything we do for him seems to go amiss. When he gets into trouble, which is often—almost every other day—we try to call him to reason, to correct him, but it's in one ear and out the other. After some troublesome situation, he would come to me with some hypothetical predicament.

"**What if this...? What if that...?**" he would often inquire.

I would usually answer to some degree of reason, but after a while of indulging in this, I said:

"**Son, this is a fruitless exercise. The variations of what can and might happen are infinite. You must see that you're the ultimate cause of what comes to you, primarily due to your way of thinking and acting. You are bound to fall into "error" no matter what wisdom I impart to you. If you don't change, "trouble" will surely find you.**"

Without proper understanding and effort of the party in question, we are just in a state of "instructing a thief on how to get away with theft." Still, by Universal Law, nobody gets away with anything. We must recognize that it is not within our power to change anyone. Notwithstanding, it is always a parent's duty to teach. Just realize that no matter your efforts or good intentions, no learning can be done for them.

One day I was in meditative prayer when mother and son started arguing. As wife and husband often do these days, they exchanged heated words like enemies. This is not a one-time thing, and it happens often. Even worse, it's been increasing in frequency, volume, and heaviness. I'm extremely fond of silence, but there always seems to be a lack of it. So, like so many times before, I came and tried to bring him to reason.

Suddenly I asked, "**Do you think we don't love you?**"

"I don't think you do," he promptly replied.

His answer didn't trigger an emotional response, but it did surprise me. I told him to elaborate on a list of what a loving parent should do. He made a simple but good list (I won't elaborate on this). I asked him to point out one thing we didn't do on that list, but he couldn't. Don't get me wrong, I don't think of ourselves as the greatest of parents. We have missed the mark and made "mistakes," but we try so hard, so many things, in so many different ways.

As I was thinking of this, I realized: *"Don't we, as God's children, act in that very same way."* Many of us believe He doesn't love us, that He neglects us: **"How can He let this and that happen? Doesn't He see what I want, what I need?"** I realize we don't know any better than a 9-year-old child.[18]

Raising a child is rarely an easy endeavor. Those of a kind, peaceful nature often expect to bring about offspring of the same spirit, but this is very rarely the case. There is almost an infinite variety of reasons that lead a soul to be born into a particular family or environment, and trying to figure out what these are is almost certainly pointless. Just be sure to know that there are no mistakes and no coincidences. All you can do is deal with what you've been given. Accept and understand your children, but more importantly, accept and understand your own limitations, which in no way means indulging anyone in anything. It's just that we are all limited in our own ability to do. Understanding and accepting this is fundamental in our living, in our doing. So, just try to do your best without falling into the same "mistakes" over and over again.

With a newborn in the family, things got even more complicated, but I cannot complain about any of it. We are the makers of our own circumstances. I took on the responsibility of taking care of the baby while my wife spent her days at work; of course, this was quite a handful.

---

[18] At the time, I understood little of the depth and intricacies of the truth behind these statements.

My wife said, "**Look, if you see that you can't handle it, will put her in a nursery. Hire someone or maybe leave her with your parents for a while?**"

I replied, "**Look, I won't trust strangers with her if I don't have to, nor will I burden others with it. We'll manage.**"

One should not abstain from doing what's right and proper just because it is difficult, and things do tend to become difficult. At such times I always remember the words of the Chinese mystic:

"Your children are not good for your work."

I've come to realize that this applies to both spiritual and material life.

I was isolating myself more and more, not intentionally. Things just seemed to flow that way, although I did avoid partaking in "bad" company. Despite my troubles and difficulties, fleeting moments of peace gave me hope. I found solace in books, too. Somehow, the right one would find its way into my hands, helping me through a particular phase of my struggle. At times glimpses of gardens and forests would come in visions, and although I didn't understand them, I always considered them auspicious.

There was an event regarding a book, which I'll relate. For some months, the bulb or socket in my living room was shot. I always used the lamp by the couch to read and didn't really feel the need to fix it. One night I was reading, standing up, when I came across a passage that I recited in my mind.

"What I give, you take."

As soon as I did, the light that hadn't worked for two months turned on and stayed on. This passage pertains to a curious event where master Yogananda gave these words as an answer. I took them as words coming from God and Guru, as one and the same.

The months passed, and the time to apply for Kriya Yoga initiation was approaching. At this point, doubts started to come before me:

"How could I be initiated by someone who is no longer of this world? Can I really be initiated by third-generation disciples? Can I be initiated by a lesson in the meantime?"

Oddly enough, books speaking ill of Kriya and institutions came to my attention almost simultaneously. I was at a crossroads but promptly decided to trust and follow my chosen path. Right about this time, the pressure from my ordeals started to decrease. For some reason that I could not see, relief began to arrive after twelve to fourteen months of ordeals.

To qualify for Kriya, one must fill out a questionnaire and pass an interview with an SRF monastic. On the day of my interview, I mentioned to the priest that I wasn't really married.

Priest – **"Oh, so you're not married."**

Me – **"Where just not married on paper. Why? Do you think it would help in the spiritual life?"**

Priest – **"Well, let me check my intuition... Yes, I think it would help you both."**

Me – **"Really? isn't it just a formality?"**

Priest – **"Well, you asked, I answered."**

We spent a significant part of our lives (19 years) living and embodying the sacrament of marriage in every way, but formally tying the knot left me conflicted. I had no desire or need of my own, nor did I want to waste money on it. That night I tossed and turned in bed, asking for a sign:

"Is this right? Does it serve a purpose?"

The next day I woke up with a great sense of joy and took it as a "Yes." We promptly arranged everything. We refurbished some old wedding rings, applied for a license, and arranged for the religious ceremony. We informed and invited all our close relatives, insisting that no gifts were necessary. A simple ceremony was held in a month, and a get-together took place in our home without pressure on guests or ourselves.

I would like to clarify that we did not make such a decision out of feeling that we were living in "sin," which is total nonsense. We did it to outwardly express something that was already inwardly true, and such an act does seem to serve a purpose in this World.

At this point, I decided to let go of all crutches. I stored my beads, cut off my long hair, and let go of rituals, chanting, incense, and candles. Even my prayers, which had been evolving over time, changed. The only support I needed was the one I already had since the beginning. Although I wasn't expecting any particular result, lo and behold, my burden became lighter, and somehow things started flowing more smoothly.

We have a tendency to complicate things, and I'm no exception. At one time, I even intended to follow many regulative principles of devotional service. Fortunately, divine wisdom showed me that I was getting into a world of difficulty. These "observances" are almost second nature to the Hindu tradition/religion, but to westerners, such regulatory directives will almost certainly become obstacles. I saw that there was no need to do these things, but the full realization of why came much later in time.

Soon after, I received my Kriya lessons and started preparing to perform the informal Kriya Initiation. I arranged everything carefully and took initiation on the 14th of November 2019. The technique, which appeared simple enough, turned out to be quite tricky. Nevertheless, I felt a coldness in my spine and a tingling feeling in my lower vertebrae. For the first time ever, I could practice with half-opened eyes. I started to practice regularly and saw that this would be quite a challenge, but despite my faulty practice, I could still see great benefits deriving from it.

A week after Initiation, a voice came to me in a dream and said: "**On the 85th day, things will be different.**" Upon waking up, I understood it to be related to Kriya. I added the numbers and thought this might be counting from this very same day or from the day I took initiation (7th of February 2020 or 14th of February 2020), so I waited.

Meanwhile, I decided to do my part and sign up for a formal Kriya Initiation. If I were to fail, it wouldn't be for lack of trying or doing. January came, and I started booking flights and arranging my stay for the upcoming event. Somehow I found it impossible. After five or six attempts, I understood that I wasn't supposed to go and arranged to be signed up for a later event in October. Soon after, reports on the Coronavirus (Covid-19) started flooding the news. This contagious virus was spreading worldwide, and one of the most afflicted countries was the same one I was trying to go to. All flights came to be canceled, which would not change for the foreseeable future.

I had an even mind about all this, but a curious thought did come to mind. *"How could a virus with such a low death rate send the world into so much chaos?"* It kind of makes you wonder.

On the 12th of February, what was promised came in a dream. I found myself in a field of bare brown land no bigger than 200 ft² (20 m²). I could not see beyond this, only darkness. I was standing, doing nothing in particular, when all of a sudden, lightning began falling all around me, getting closer and closer. I started moving, trying to evade it as if I could.

Shortly after trying to escape these strikes, a lightning bolt descended straight from the sky, hitting me on the crown of the head and going through my spine into the Earth. The event seemed to occur in slow motion as lightning pierced through my spine, cascading downward in circular expansions of light and energy blasting from the core of my chakras. I could tell that the expansion emanating from my head was the most significant (20 cm or 8 inches in radius), and the others were much smaller.

With regards to color, the pure white light emanating from my head left an impression, but the others, not so much. I recall seeing red, orange, and yellow, perhaps, but I cannot say for certain and prefer not to guess. The time dilation aided somewhat in my seeing, but things still happened pretty fast.

Right after this "striking" experience, I opened my eyes. I immediately felt that something was different, that this meant something, although I did not know what. You may have noticed that the date doesn't quite add up, so let me explain why. The days given were reporting 85 days of practice, and since I was sick for a couple of days (two), it fits just right.

Two months after this event, another "dream" came to me. Although I'm not sure, it was a dream, for I wasn't unconscious. It had what appeared to be a physical expression and, at the same time, moved my consciousness. While lying in bed, I started feeling that deep relaxation that precedes sleep. I then perceived a voice coming from my crown chakra. At first, the voice was faint, but as I "pushed," as if I were forcing myself through a door made of elastic material, the voice became louder and louder. As I broke through, the voice stopped, and I opened my eyes.

I didn't understand a word, but I could almost immediately and consciously know that it was master Yogananda speaking in a tone much like in a lecture. I believe this was given to me in this way so that I would take it as an auspicious sign, which I did. Paramahansa Yogananda's voice was the only saintly voice I knew. Were it any other, I would almost undoubtedly start to question the nature of this experience—which was not its intended purpose.

After a few months, the nature of this experience was revealed by a similar one: One day, I woke up quite clear-minded in the middle of the night. It was way too early to start the day, so I went to the bathroom and returned promptly to bed. Shortly after, I began to hear voices. Whispers. They were coming from within, calling, but I could not tell what was being said. As I took conscious awareness of these sounds, I felt an overwhelming vibration taking over my body. Without thought, I said, *"Help me, Mother."* I don't know why I articulated things this way, but as soon as I did, I felt a hand pulling me by the arm, peeling me like a sticker from my body.

As I felt myself hovering mid-air, I thought of opening my eyes, which led me to return to my body. These sounds and vibrations are preludes to out-of-body experiences, and they can be nurtured and intensified to some degree if you so wish.

Almost two years have passed since I started this journey, my mind is more peaceful, and the heaviness/stiffness in my body has significantly subsided. At times I can actually manage to sleep, and my practice has improved. I don't force anything anymore. However long or short my practice is, I take it as it comes, and if, at times, things seem not to go so well, I pay no heed to it. Things will be better tomorrow or the next day.

The Life and Spiritual Journey of No One

Chapter Thirteen

The End or a New Beginning

In the beginning, I stated that if this book managed to help just one, I would consider its purpose fulfilled, and although I stand by what I said, it just might be that the one it helped is me. Even though I didn't write this book for myself, I was mostly compelled to do it. Now, I find myself in a better place. Understanding and acknowledging the divine presence in my life has put me in a higher state of mind, a higher state of being. Perhaps that's part of what we have to do, albeit through different ways and means. Because of this, I felt that whatever the outcome, this book had already fulfilled its purpose by helping me.

I wrote all I could or all I was allowed to write and felt that there was definitely something worth sharing with the world. I then decided to do everything I could to put things in finished form. With that in mind, I asked my sister Sara, a graduate in foreign languages, to revise the book and share her insights. She did, and I will transcribe what transpired:

"Just before the weekend, my brother asked me to read and proofread a book he had written. At the time, I was struggling with some issues and had no intention of reading it right away, but on that very night, a vivid dream changed my mind.

"I was sitting with my brother and his wife in a place that looked like a conference room. Opposite us were three others, but who they were, I cannot say. It felt like a business meeting but not as formal. My brother's wife got down to business. She eloquently stated that there would be a book launch very soon and handed things over to my brother. He politely declined and redirected the request to me. In the dream, I was aware that I hadn't read the book yet. Somehow I managed to articulate what I thought my brother wanted to convey through this book—its purpose—and everyone seemed happy with the explanation.

"What struck me as quite interesting about this dream was how confident and business-like my brother's wife was. She exuded a strong and assertive masculine energy, words I wouldn't normally ascribe to her. Conversely, my brother had a very feminine energy—more passive, calm, accepting, and peaceful. I felt this was not yet the time to publish this book. I also thought that this new persona was still in the process of being birthed and that the book would have to account for the road yet untraveled for it to be complete."

After reading the book, she said that it was incomplete. She felt that there would be other chapters to be written and that a different arrangement would be given to the final product. I understood and accepted what was being conveyed through my sister, but I had nothing else to write. So I let the book rest while dwelling in thoughts of how many years it would take for such things to come into being.

A while after, something started appearing in my mind. I've been avoiding writing about it, for I knew not where it came from. It wasn't a dream or a vision. *"Was it my imagination?"* I don't think so. One thing you should realize about me is that I'm terrible at imagining things. Often, certain practices imply visualization and imagination, but to me, these are just exercises in frustration. Either I see something, or I don't. There is no forcing it.

Over and over, thoughts/images of this were striking my mind. *"How could I write about something if I knew not where it came from?"* Suddenly these words came into my mind: *"It's a memory."* Immediately, my heart bumped. **Yes. Yes.**

I was kneeling by the side of a bed. Laying on it was One who I believed to be Krishna. I saw not His face, for I was facing His feet, and my sight ranged only up to His knees. He appeared to be wearing yellow silk pants, and His skin was of a strange dark color. I cannot really tell what color it was. It seemed to be more than one. It definitely had some kind of gray and one other, also dark in nature. Together, they seemed to form a pattern of sorts.

The soles of His feet were covered with particles of gold. Much like wet feet are laid with sand on the beach. I took a portion of it with two fingers. Holding my hand up, I cascaded these particles before my eyes. How entranced was I at the sight of these falling particles that, at times, flickered like stars.

This memory came to its conclusion with the sight of particles pouring into my mind's eye. I realized this was not my memory. This was part of the Creative record, and for some reason, I was allowed to share in it—to experience it as my own.

As it turns out, this ushered in some clarity on the things I had to do. As a result, the final part of this book began to unravel (Part III), grow, and change step by step.

The Life and Spiritual Journey of No One

Chapter Fourteen

Work and My Longing to Help Others

I was feeling much more comfortable with my spiritual practice. Letting go of the chains of control that had held sway over me certainly helped. I felt a flow of change within myself, something moving toward something greater. If this would lead me somewhere, or nowhere at all, I did not know. It was one more unknown in a life already filled with uncertainty.

On this journey, I've received the answers to so many questions. However, a few still elude me: "What kind of work should I do? What expression will my spiritual journey take? Can I do anything to help it along?" These were points where I seemed to have no help at all. I kept waiting for a voice to guide me and answer my questions, but nothing came—not even a yes or a no.

Work

I was becoming unsure of what to do. A few years prior, I had ventured into trading, which was quite a daunting endeavor. Was I supposed to give it up? Let me give you some background on this.

In the beginning, I started alone, trying to learn as much as I could through whatever resources I could find. These were few in number and soon dried up. I knew there were many unsavory characters ready to take advantage, but I had to learn from someone, so I tried to find courses on the subject—which I did. Everything was really expensive, some online, others in person. After some research and reviews, I decided to go to London and participate in a weekend course given by a trading company.

Even before taking the course, I was told I would need a laptop, a funded account with a broker of their choosing, and to sign up for a platform service that allowed me to receive data, view charts, and analyze price movement. Curiously enough, I was only told of these facts after paying. None of it made any sense.

"Why did I have to fund an account when I knew very little—**if anything at all—**about trading? Why that particular broker? Why did I have to pay for a service to see charts and prices when I could do it for free anywhere else?"

I wrote an email demanding a refund of my money, to which they responded promptly with a phone call.

Caller – **"Hello. Mr. ...?"**

Me – **"Yes."**

Caller – **"My name is ... and I'm calling from ... (the company). I see in your email that you want a refund."**

Me – **"Yes."**

Caller – **"Can I ask why?"**

Me – **"I find no good reason to do the things you are asking your students to do. I know very little about trading. Shouldn't one learn first before doing any trading?**

Caller – **"The platform service has the strategies we use embedded in it, so you receive the signals without making much in the way of analysis, and you are getting this service at a discount because of us. Regarding the broker, you can use another, but our manual is based on the interface of that broker, and you have benefits through our company.**

"Everything is pretty much done for you. It's easy." (he said in confidence). "You just have to enter the trade once you receive the signal, and that's it. What are you afraid of?"

Me – "Nothing. I cannot really say anything without knowing these things in detail."

Caller – "**I do these things myself. You'll see there is nothing to worry about.**"

Me – "**OK.**" (I wasn't convinced, but I had nothing to base my doubts on, so I gave him the benefit of the doubt.)

Caller – "**OK, Mr. ... see you then. Have a nice day.**"

The day came, and there were quite a lot of people in the room—thirty to thirty-five. Seeing that each had paid somewhere between £1,000 to £1,600, I started doing my math. Having done so, I thought that £40,000, to give a round number, is rather good pay for a weekend's worth of work.

There were only two traders giving the class, and there wasn't much of a class to speak of. The first day was just a recounting of their life stories and a whole lot of boasting. They continually emphasized the importance of starting early and with as much money as one can possibly muster, as we were to risk only 1% of our funds in each trade.[19]

This was nothing more than crazy talk to my ears, far from being sound advice, but I kept quiet and listened, and the day went by without much learning being made. On the morning of the second day, we seemed to be following the same pattern as the first. When suddenly, a certain figure entered the room. A well-dressed man holding a glass of whiskey approached and sat grinningly in the corner of a table, waiting to be introduced. He was said to be a highly successful trader who fancied wearing £5,000 underwear and other such garments.

---

[19] Often, they would say to turn into money as much of our assets as we possibly could, to endeavor to earn as much as we could.

There was little learning and a whole lot of boasting. He kept saying that we had to seize the opportunities in life once they were given and that we would soon receive such an offer. After some more boasting, we were led into a room to see a power-point presentation. We saw a neatly arranged table, a buffet, champagne, and other neat and fine little items, but no one could touch them. Here we were given the opportunity to join a VIP Traders club. Those who joined would be eligible to have a professional trader to teach and trade with them, but not without receiving a cut of their earnings. They would also become privy to yacht parties, premiers, and other fancy perks. "**All this could be yours for a lifetime membership fee of £35,000.**"

I was surprised, but most of the others were angry, and with good reason. A few though (three) stepped forward and, having signed a formal contract, received a fancy pen, drank champagne, and ate caviar while most of us watched in disbelief at this surreal scenario.

In the afternoon, we finally touched on the subject of trading, but this was done in such a light manner that I could not tell if anything of worth was given. They set as a requirement to undertake the course all those things I mentioned above, yet we didn't even touch the computer they so eloquently said we needed.

We browsed through four or five pages of a very thick manual and vaguely touched on the subject of strategies and placing trades. Most students were happy, but I was pretty unsure about all this. Much study was required before I could state anything as fact.

After a few weeks, I realized we'd been taught just enough to lose all our money. Without going into technical details, the strategies were ineffective as a whole. Going back and forth between services didn't help, and the crudeness of the broker's interface was such that trades were extremely difficult to place and manage. Even the encyclopedia-sized manual had no real value. It was filled with pictures and oversized lettering, with very little content—not worth the paper it was printed on.

This experience made me even more aware of those who prey in this field of business. Eventually, I was led to a "good" teacher who taught me sound trading. I even created my own strategy, which worked with incredible precision.

Things seemed to be going well, but after some success, things changed. I can say that the market wasn't particularly favorable, but most strategies had a 60% success rate. What was uncanny was that I managed to miss every single one of them. Every trade I made was a loss.

Statistically speaking, even if I entered random trades, I would have shown some profit on at least some of them. What seemed to be a statistical improbability became my reality. So much so that I almost lost all my previous gains.

Acknowledging the course of events, I thought I was being blocked for some reason. There was a lesson here, but I couldn't figure it out. I was always opposed to the idea of allowing others to run my capital. So I thought I was being told, in a way, not to spend my time doing such work and to trust it to the hands of others, and so I did.

The result: On the very first week, I lost all my previous gains and then some. What seemed to be improbable—taking into account the trader's history—actually happened. I could have continued but decided to take the hint and stop everything.

The Universe often tries to keep us from doing what we shouldn't, but we often ignore the signs. We insist and persist, which in turn leads the Universe to kick back even harder. This fact has played out throughout my life, so now I strive to listen a little better, and so should you.

I was left somewhat disoriented at the time: *"Am I to do nothing? Something else? What?"*

Magic

I've always wanted to help others ever since I can remember, but I was unsure of how to do it. For most of my life, I focused on transient forms of help that, although right in themselves, had only marginal effects on this world and its people. Lingering within me was a longing to heal others, but how to do it still escaped me. Upon entering the spiritual path, the desire to express physical healing grew within me, to do as Jesus and others had done. Still, time made me impatient, which led me to become interested in "magic." This was quite the conundrum. I was interested in "magic," but I also had a bias against it since I was led to misuse it in a past life. As you can understand, I was always reluctant to look at such works, even if my intentions were good. Understanding that this derived primarily from fear, I decided to face it.

I knew there was an incredible amount of rubbish out there but was surprised to find, even without looking, an unbelievable abundance of books on black magic. This was not what I was aiming for, so I kept going, looking for those speaking of white or sacred magic. I was somewhat astonished, and knowing what I know now, I saw embedded in most works very subtle ways of deceit. An almost imperceptible mix of positive and negative. Still, in some, this deception was more blatant and in your face. Mind you, I am speaking of books that claim to be of good nature.

Most of these workings demand lengthy and complex rituals that must be performed on point. But what I would like to make you aware of is that when you bid, demand, or seek to control any entity, you are working through the ways of the negative. What also came as a shock was that even the nature of the one being asked/controlled seemed completely overlooked. Everything was considered fine just as long as the work got done. Like I said before, this could take very subtle forms going on undetected in books that appear to be "good," but at times, there are red flags that, due to their more explicit nature, should make one stay on guard. However, sometimes some "sound" reasoning is given to justify their use.

Example: In one such book, it is said that angels are more powerful than demons and that we should use the angels to control the demons to do our bidding. This is done in order to do work in the material world, emphasizing that there is no other way to do it.

We live in such a crazy world that this might pass as truth, but let's look at this in some detail. It is stated that the angels are more powerful than the demons and that they can subdue them; no contradiction here. Then it is said that only through demons can one work in the material world. How can one who is more powerful than the other not be able to do what the lesser can? Bear in mind that this undertaking aims for good works and service for the overall good, not to harm others or for personal gain/power.

On the other hand, there are many grades of light and shades of dark. To say in a linear way that one is stronger than the other is a somewhat erroneous statement. Do understand that everything in material creation comes from Light/Love and that only through our free choice can those of a brighter or darker nature be "born."

Be also cautious of such books that say:

"... *do this in Fear of the Lord.*" or "... *remember, the most important thing is to Fear God above all things.*"

The ways of fear are not the ways of the light, and since all things come from Love, it seems curious to reach Him or serve Him by ways of fear.

I cannot say that I dwelled in depth into this subject due to the "heaviness" of such work, but even so, I would say that I got a pretty good feel for them. Again, I emphasize that these were books acclaimed to be good and sacred. I then decided not to involve myself with such workings or any other type of meaningless pursuits.

Hypnosis

Suddenly, I thought I was going about this in the wrong way. If I already had this knowledge, why look for it anywhere else? I admit that I always had a negative impression of hypnosis for various reasons. Still, at this point, regressive hypnosis seemed to be my best option, and I could not go on thinking that I did not succeed because I hadn't done everything possible. I found someone with experience very close to "home" and decided to trust her. I was somewhat fearful, but not of being hypnotized or facing any potential past darkness. What I was truly afraid of was bringing back any negative influence. She said this might happen if hypnosis was wrongly done, but she had a great deal of experience with such cases. Curiously enough, this reassurance was only given after the deed was done. It provided little comfort then.

The first step was to look at my chart. She seemed somewhat disconcerted, which, in turn, led her to pause for moments of quiet introspection. What she said next was much like what I'd been told so many times before. She just told it in a way that bore even more weight of responsibility on my shoulders. Regarding this subject, I would like to say this: No one soul can change this world. We just strive, as we should, to build on each other's service. There have been so many who have worked in this world and beyond it to achieve a great purpose. So many souls of light work together, striving to instill change for the benefit of all. Still, I am always left with the feeling that this world cares not for it.

After a moment's pause, we began our session. At this point, I would also like to add that I was never wholly unconscious. This hypnotic process aims only to slightly put aside the conscious mind so that all other things might surface.

She asked me to imagine a safe place, to which I automatically responded by placing myself on a beach I'd seen in dreams. She then verbalized some dates and told me to see if any were important. In my estimate, they were all pretty recent, most of them from the past millennium. Only two were what we might call older, 25 AD and 500 BC, but none of them really stirred anything within me.

Me – "No, there's nothing there."

Hypnotist – "That's OK. As you step forward, you will walk back in time into a life of significance.

"Look at your feet. What do you see?"

Me – "I see some sort of sandals."

They seemed ornamented in some way.

Hypnotist – "What are you wearing?"

Me – "I'm not sure, some sort of tunic, maybe?"

Hypnotist – "What's your name?"

Everything was really faint and blurry. At this point, I began shaking like bamboo leaves.

Me – "I don't know."

Hypnotist – "Where are you? What are you doing?"

Me – "Somewhere barren, like a desert. I seem to be going for a walk."

Hypnotist – "How old are you?"

Me – "Twenty, twenty-five, I'm not sure."

Hypnotist – "Now go to a time of key importance in this life... Where are you?"

Me – "I don't know. I see walls made of large blocks of stone all around me.

Hypnotist – "**Is there someone there? What are you doing?**"

Me – "**I feel alone. I don't know what I'm doing, a test maybe.**"

Hypnotist – "**Test of what?**"

Me – "**I don't know.**"

Everything was so narrow, faint, and fuzzy that I couldn't tell anymore.

Hypnotist – "**OK, let's go back in time to your childhood. What do you see?**"

Me – "**I'm playing outside a house in a garden.**"

I intuitively felt that this house was somewhat above average but not too ostentatious.

Hypnotist – "**How old are you?**"

Me – "**I'm not sure, somewhere between seven and ten.**"

I was wearing a knee-high tunic with some drawings/figures in it. I had short spiky hair, and I seemed pretty happy.

Hypnotist – "**Is there someone at the house?**"

Me – "**I don't know, but I feel like my mother is there.**"

Hypnotist – "**Go there, and look at her.**"

At this point, I started shaking even more.

Me – "**I can't see.**"

Hypnotist – "**Who is she?**"

Me – "**I don't know.**"

The hypnotist got up and placed something on my forehead. For some reason, I began to see much more clearly from there on out.

Hypnotist – "OK, let's move forward into manhood. How old are you?"

Me – "About 25 years old."

I was dressed much in the same way but in a simpler and more serious attire made of "plain" white linen. I was also wearing a linen headpiece with some sort of pattern at the front.

Hypnotist – "Where are you?"

Me – "In a garden. In a courtyard that gives entry to a great building."

Hypnotist – "A palace?"

Me – "Maybe."

Hypnotist – "Enter it. What do you see?"

Me – "A great hall with large pillars of stone on each side. There is a door at the other end."

Hypnotist – "Is there anyone there."

Me – "No, but someone was working in the garden outside."

Hypnotist – "Go in and see if you can find someone important."

Me – "I see a child about 10 years old, my son."

This was an incredibly clear picture. The boy was sitting on his mother's lap, but I could not see her face, only her robes. The child seemed so happy. He was wearing little in the way of clothes, only a kilt. He had gold bracelets on his wrists and a wide necklace on his chest that seemed made out of orange stone encased in gold. His eyes were accentuated by black paint, and his head was neatly shaved except for what I might call a folded ponytail protruding from the top of his head. Holding it in place were two golden rings evenly spaced apart.

Hypnotist – **"Who is he in this lifetime?"**

Me – **"My son, maybe."**

I said this because my current son is now 10, but honestly, I do not feel this to be true.

Hypnotist – **"Can you tell me what you do for a living?"**

Me – **"I'm not sure. I feel that I don't have to do much of anything to earn my keep."**

Hypnotist – **"OK. So let's go to a place where you perform some sort of work. What do you see?"**

Me – **"I am sitting in a large room but not on a chair."**

Hypnotist – **"Is it a throne?"**

Me – **"Maybe."**

It certainly looked like a throne. One made of polished stone, but I didn't want to say it aloud.

Hypnotist – **"What are you doing?"**

Me – **"Judgment. A man is kneeling before me. He is afraid."**

He was a bald man of brown complexion. He was very nicely dressed, much more so than me, and his robes had color.

Hypnotist – **"What did he do? Who is he?"**

Me – **"I'm not sure. I feel the man to be someone of importance and that he had abused his power somehow."**

I don't know if I was directed, but I moved into a great balcony. I was overlooking a great city that stood radiant with a great river passing in the background. If you haven't guessed already, I was in ancient Egypt. Of all places in this session, this sight was the one that filled me with peace. I kept shaking but a little less so.

Over the setting sun of the evening, I saw temples, obelisks, houses of noble standing, neat roads, water channels, and pools. I did not see the great pyramids, but I think there were pyramid-like structures. This didn't look at all like the barren Egypt I had imagined. It was alive in many ways, filled with gardens and palm trees.

After reporting what I was seeing, she said:

"**Let's go now to the time of your death. What do you see?**"

Me – "**I'm lying in bed with a fever, sweating.**"

Hypnotist – "**How old are you?**"

Me – "**I'm about 56, and I'm looking compassionately at someone.**"

I had a few gray hairs evenly spread out through my head.

Hypnotist – "**Look back at your life and forgive any wrong you might have done.**"

Me – "**There was nothing wrong. It was a good life.**"

She said to take any gifts from this life and return to my safe place. She then asked me to see a great light above me, to see myself being drawn by it, and to meet my spiritual guide(s).

Hypnotist – "**Who do you see?**"

Me – "**Krishna.**"

I immediately knew it was Him. He was surrounded by light that partially and unevenly covered His figure from my sight. He was beautiful, dark blue, with full reddish lips and luscious long hair. I cannot properly describe His attire. I do remember a very curious cone-shaped crown that appeared to be made out of gold.

Hypnotist – "**Ask Him what you want.**"

Me – **"What do I have to do?"**

Hypnotist – **"What did he say?"**

Me – **"He just smiled."**

Hypnotist – **"Ask Him what you must do at this moment in time?"**

I did, and as an answer, He made a brushing motion to the side. I took it as a sign to clear myself of all the mental garbage and clutter that had built up over the years. I've made some strides in this but clearly there was still much to get rid of.

"Ask Him what sign to look for to know if something is right."

I did, and as an answer, His arm moved upward with a straight hand to touch the spiritual center between the eyebrows.

"Okay, let's fall back."

"You are alone in a peaceful place, and in front of you there's a tree."

I immediately saw a big oak tree and felt an irresistible urge to touch it. I reached out, and it began to grow, expanding to planetary proportions. The ground quaked beneath me, and I gazed up in awe. I'm fairly certain that my expression of astonishment was visible, but what she said next discouraged me from discussing it.

"Reach out and touch the tree. Know that you are that tree. Sense the gentle breeze rustling through the leaves, relish in the comforting shade it provides, and explore the rugged texture of its trunk. Be at peace for you are one."

Once again, a sense of humility held me back from uttering a word. However, I eventually came to realize that concealing what I had seen and felt in this and other experiences would serve no purpose.

Shortly after, the session was over, and so was my shaking. I asked if this was normal. She said, "**No, you hold a lot of fear regarding something.**"

After asking me about my time of birth, she stated that I lived in Atlantis (or Atlanta), which did not surprise me in the least. I had an overwhelming feeling that I've been around for quite some time, and I've stopped seeing this as a bad thing, but only recently. This was not the session I was expecting. I thought I would be brought into a dark time and place, but this was not the case, and she was pretty honest and upfront. She said:

"**Look, we could drag this out, but this is not the way for you. All you need is within you. You just have to overcome this fear that stops you.**"

She advised some methods of overcoming, but I already had an answer. I just didn't know how long it would take to get there.

The desire to express divine healing continued for a while, but I came to see and understand a few things by divine grace. Firstly, all human beings have the power to heal themselves, physically or otherwise. Secondly, there are many forms of physical healing. Can anyone say that one is better than the other if they accomplish the same goal? Thirdly, without change, physical healing, be it divine or not, serves no real purpose, for we are bound to be sick again, to suffer, die and repeat. Lastly, accepting this form of service binds one to the commitment of fulfilling its purpose. There would be no turning back. I could see the circus playing out in my head, a healer to some, entertainment to others, and a source of income to a few. Any higher purpose would be lost.

For enlightened souls, divine healing is not an end in itself. It serves as a precursor to a higher purpose, so often, such expressions are small in number. One might say that Jesus did more than most, many divine workings in fact, but was this because he loved his "brother" more than any other enlightened soul? No, of course not. They all share the same Love, and the same goal. What truly differs is their form of service, nothing more.

The Life and Spiritual Journey of No One

Chapter Fifteen

Spiritual Cross Road

At this point, I was pretty overwhelmed by the number of techniques in my practice. There were so many that quite some time was needed to perform them without hastening the process. On average, I spent more than two hours in practice twice a day, morning and evening. Not to mention more extended periods that should be performed at least once a week. Doing all these things in this day and age can be quite challenging, especially for those with jobs, spouses, children, etc. Everyone's situation is different, but something is bound to give when trying to do so much.

For over a year, I was pretty consistent in my Kriya practice, but without any review, I was pretty unsure of what I was doing. Despite any faulty practice, I was still seeing some definite benefits from it, but the truth is that as time went by, I felt more and more stuck in a rut that seemed to be leading nowhere. In a spiritual moment of inspiration, my sister Sara reached out, conveying a truth told to me many times before:

Sara – "**Remember what you've been told. For you, these techniques are distractions more than anything else.**"

Me – "**Should I stop them?**"

Sara – "**Yes.**"

Me – "**Should I stop Kriya also.**"

Sara – "**Kriya in the right state can be of a monumental difference, but stopping, for now, is in your best interest. If something seems off, why do you do it? Remember, there's great wisdom dwelling within you.**"

I was having a really hard time with this. Again and again, emphasis was put that this was the way and that there should be no deviations. On top of it all was the vow I made to continue no matter what. I was struck by fear and doubt, but I ultimately had to recognize this truth. I only asked for a sign to know when to resume practice (Kriya).

I stopped using techniques almost immediately. The only exception was the Energization Exercises, which I deemed helpful. Meditation was still a part of my life, and to my surprise, by doing almost nothing, I was already "there." The flow of life force was very much alive in my spine and brain. Most of the time, my breath was "short" or nonexistent, like I was being sustained by some "other" source.

I changed my morning practice to an hour around noon. Techniques notwithstanding, I found this time to be most auspicious, and I believe this to be due to a factor of "light." I began looking into mantras and discerned that the most auspicious ones were the Vasudeva and Gayatri mantras, but for some reason, the first was always closer to my heart.

After practice, I began performing a yogic pose named Savasana (corpse pose). At the time, I did not know its name. I was just striving to practice stillness and detachment from the body, and somehow, it felt right. In time all these things increased the quantity and quality of the energy flowing in my spine and brain.

After a few months, an e-mail came inviting me to an online Kriya class, which I immediately took as a blatant sign to resume practice. I continued my practice for over a year until I felt it was time to apply for the second Kriya. In truth, I wasn't sure I needed it, but without knowledge of it, how could I be sure?

I applied and was immediately shut down. In a very short call, I was told I should be following the prescribed path. I tried to explain the how and the why, but to no effect. In my journey, I often felt that we put ourselves in spiritual boxes that prevent us from acting freely, especially in our interactions with others. This is also very true within a spiritual organization which is just another box of a different size but a box nevertheless.

I would like to believe that things were not intended to turn out this way. Notwithstanding, I still think this organization ends up helping many. I believe these limitations sprout not from any ill intent, but out of an imprinted sense of service that inadvertently tends to bind and confine.

Sometimes I would reach out to SRF for help, but despite all good intentions, no help came. It all seemed scripted, fixed in a certain way of thinking and doing. Shouldn't we be working to become free? Isn't this the true nature of our journey?

The monastic expressed his position, but I was unwilling to turn back from what seemed right, nor was I willing to lie in an application for my own benefit. As such, I accepted that I would have to content myself with this first Kriya for the rest of my life and that this would have to do.

To my great surprise, this knowledge was revealed to me the very next day. What seemed impossible actually happened. Along with the second Kriya came the first, in its unadulterated form. Up until now, I had no idea that Paramahansa Yogananda had altered the techniques to better suit the needs of westerners.

Generally speaking, it is quite common for a master to tweak certain techniques if they deem these changes to be of beneficial. True masters are not stuck in fixed ways of thinking or doing. How unfortunate would it be to deny entry into a particular path just due to one's inability to do a certain thing(s)?

I understand SRF's position in teaching in a certain way, but this form of acting has some very clear limitations that will almost certainly arouse mixed feelings in their students.

Now, how I came to acquire this is not important. What surprised me was that some of these practices were ones I was already doing of my own accord. I also thought rather uncanny that a series of circumstances in my life led me to perform movements very similar to yogic jewels like Talabya Kriya and Khechari mudra.[20]

By now, I should be used to these synchronicities, but these Universal arrangements never cease to amaze me.

I could now see some present and future add-ons regarding techniques. This begs the question: How much time will one need to do all these things? Those living the life of a householder will almost certainly see their struggles increase and not the other way around. Indeed, something(s) has to be sacrificed in order to follow, to the letter, the path given by the Self-Realization Fellowship.

Monastics would often say that the sacrifice is well worth it. I understand what they mean. I felt it, lived it. I would have given everything to get it back. I would even renounce the world, but that's not the point of our existence. Some may come to choose the life of a renunciant, but we were meant to weave and interact with the world we live in. You have but to decide how to go about it.

Balance is crucial, and it implies different things for different people, so you'll just have to find your own. Can you spend two to three hours, twice a day, practicing and still have a balanced life? If you do, and it works, that's great, but many probably don't. Many people can't even handle long periods of practice. I am one such example.

My mind and spirit can handle more, but my body still lags behind. To perform Kriya properly, your body, mind, and spirit have to be in a certain state of quiet. Most of the time, I'm already there. I just try to deepen that state a little more before any higher practice.

Do you already linger in a state of stillness? How much so? What helps you deepen it? Do you need so many things and so much time to get there? You will find that different things will work faster and better for different

---

[20] Khechary mudra is a technique that consists in curling the tongue's tip back into the mouth upward into the nasal cavity. Talabya Kriya is just an exercise that aids the practitioner in achieving full control over the previous technique.

people, so try to find what's best for you. I saw myself "walking" in larger strides through the combination of old and new (Lahiri's Kriya).

Now I strive to have at least a moment to myself (in the evening), and if I can, if life allows it, I try to have another (at noon). That is my balance.

My intent is not to aggravate anyone, especially those "satisfied" in strictly following the path given by the Self-Realization Fellowship. I just acknowledge the struggles of many as well as my own. But if you are truly "satisfied," why are you still reading? Why are you still searching? Be honest with yourself. But if you have found your place, I'm happy for you. May we all be so "lucky."[21]

Struggle - Obstacles and Results

For some years now, I have lived in a constant state of struggle, as nothing seems to go my way. A barrage of difficulties and obstacles is all I see. I long to live a simple life, but despite my best efforts to minimize my responsibilities to the world, I always seem to get entangled in its workings.

To clarify, my intent is not to run away from the world. I just want to simplify an already very complex "reality" without adding to it.

We try to be wise in our spending, always attempting to save what little we can, but a barrage of problems seems to keep coming, one after the other. The various situations are not the problem; they are bound to come in life, and one should not ignore them, but I've been dealing nonstop with so many of them, and at times, with already addressed issues.

Despite my best efforts, we've been bleeding money by the thousands, but what troubled me was not the spending. Money serves its purpose, and one should use it if needed. What really bothered me was the results derived from addressing those issues. As with all things I do, I always try to address

---

[21] Luck is not a factor, it's just an expression, our will in the other hand is of a fundamental importance.

every problem with the most care and attention. But no matter how diligent, well-informed, cautious, or wise I may have been, things always seemed to turn out "badly." At times, I would see myself addressing the same issue two or three times over again.

For quite a while, I couldn't understand it. Why was everything so difficult? Should I be dismissive? Should I not care? Of course not. In every "failure," there were always lessons to be learned, but the greatest one was this: despite your best efforts, you still have no control over the outcome.

All you can do is address what comes next, always doing your best with evenness of mind, and what comes just might be the very same thing. Ultimately, I had to break free from expectations. No matter how hard I tried, control over any outcome would always escape me. I just had to accept it.

The only things we can truly aspire to control in this life are our thoughts and actions.

Chapter Sixteen

Connecting - Energy, Light, and Our Chakras

I have been sporadically describing the energy flowing to my head without really knowing what it meant. This energy would usually stay focused on my spiritual center or on the crown of my head. At most, it would spread out, swirling across my skull, but at a certain point, I began perceiving leaks of energy coming from my face. I was surprised to see that, along with this perception, burn marks started to appear. Over time, they worsened as the flow of upward energy seemed to grow more and more. I got somewhat worried. I'd already eased up on my practice, but things kept getting worse.

It is not uncommon for those on this path to experience leaks of "energy," but this was off the charts. My face looked terrible, and ordinary things like shaving and cleaning became quite painful, but shaving was the worst. I felt the need for some guidance, and as a result, part of the answer came in a vision:

Suddenly, my inner vision cleared. I saw myself going through the wall of my body, but instead of seeing blood, guts, and organs, everything seemed to be made of crystalline honeycomb structures with very curious colors. Amber is the tone that comes to mind, but there was also a reddish tone to the center of each unit.

It seemed as if a path was being opened for me to see what lay ahead. It appeared to be a small cave with an upper shaft. It resembled the shape of a Florence flask. I could see little up the shaft, for I was looking somewhat from afar. However, fitting nicely into this shape was a campfire, the logs very neatly arranged into a cone, from which blazed forth a blue fire with flickers of yellow.

I could tell that this fire was blazing in my root chakra and that all these crystalline structures served as insulation, providing protection against whatever force might pass through.

I was once told that success in this path was mostly due to a state of mind. This is true but not the complete truth. There are different measures of success, of course, but in effect, our whole being has to be made ready: body, mind, and spirit (see Appendix I). I saw part of the answer in my vision, but the rest would only come later.

We speak so much about energy and vibrations on this path that we miss what's important. In essence, most yogic techniques/practices aim to promote the flow and focus of light, primarily through our centers of consciousness — the chakras. Our understanding of light has grown somewhat, but there are still many who only acknowledge what they can see and others, only what they can measure. Light is of an unfathomable nature, and one should never circumscribe it to what the eyes can see or what an instrument can measure.

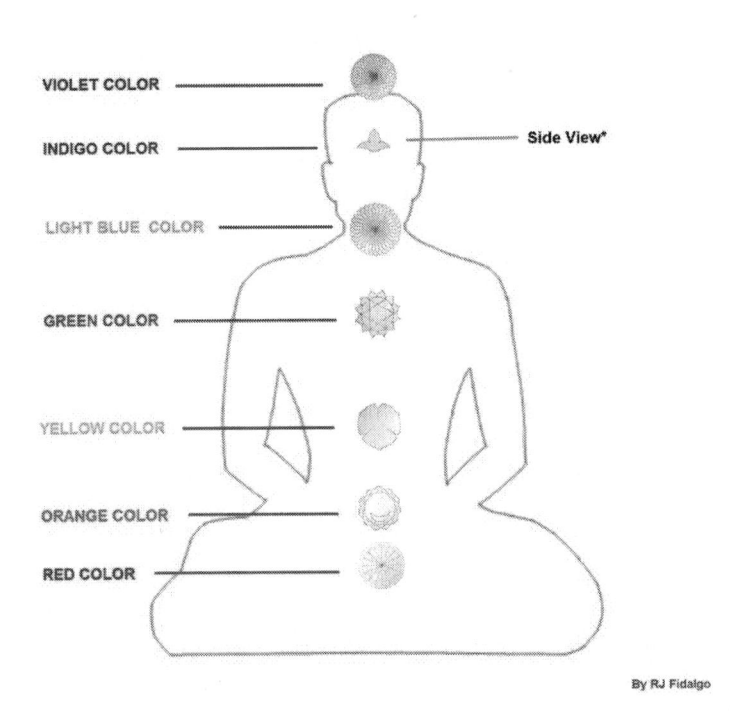

VIOLET COLOR
INDIGO COLOR — Side View*
LIGHT BLUE COLOR
GREEN COLOR
YELLOW COLOR
ORANGE COLOR
RED COLOR

By RJ Fidalgo

Picture 6º - The seven centers: Chakras

* - Most chakra depictions are given from an aerial view. My personal depiction of these centers follows that same perspective, with the exception of the sixth chakra, for I thought it might be of benefit to at least some of you. This is said to be a two-petal chakra, but this is a matter of perspective. There are, in fact, three petals, and connecting their points should result in a perfect triangle. Mine was done by hand, so it's not perfect at all.

Generally speaking, in our human experience, only the first three centers (chakras) are truly active. Usually unbalanced and broken in some way or form. As we progress, the higher centers awaken, and we move in larger strides to heal and balance. In time, our metaphysical centers (chakras) will grow to become well-defined crystalline shapes through which light will pass "unobstructed."

The flow of light is conditioned by the purity of the crystals within one's self. One should understand that perfection is not a requirement, but a certain threshold should be overcome to achieve a measure of success.

Some of you might have heard about the thousand-petal lotus, the seventh chakra located at the crown of the head. This seventh center (chakra) is just a projection of the previous six that, once completed, opens the gateway to establish a much more stable connection to the One.

My rather uncomfortable experience lasted for almost two years, and it was mostly due to an incomplete process of form and insulation.

To many, this may seem a little out there, unfathomable, but I assure you that this is just a part of a very universal process, and by the end of this book, you will have a greater understanding of it. In my process, I was never truly apart from the One I was seeking, but only after four years was I able to get back a measure of that presence.

I came to understand why it could've happened sooner, but more importantly, I understood why it didn't. There were a few reasons behind this, but the most important one was that doing so would have validated so much garbage that still lingered in my mind, and that would not do.

I must admit that the result of my process was somewhat different than I expected.

I guess we were not meant to live in a constant state of ecstasy. If that were the case, it would be rather hard to be and deal with this world. Nonetheless, my connection will continue to grow and deepen over the coming years, but at this point, a certain story ends, and a different one begins — just not one for this book.

Chapter Seventeen

Clarity, "Impossibility," Future

Many questions have been answered in my journey of consciousness, and only very few remain, but those very few are the ones that would give direction in life. What could I do? What could I bring into this world? This was a very slow, painful process, for I could not see it. Opening an Ashram seemed like something completely out of my financial ability.

On the other hand, would such an endeavor be any different from what so many are already doing? Would I do it any better? Suddenly, some clarity came to mind, and I saw a very pressing need in this world. This need gave meaning to all that I went through in life. I see that need in my children. I see it in others. The need to give/teach a sense of Universal Citizenship to all, and those who read this book will understand precisely what I mean.

Living and acting rightly in this material world is quite a venture. So this teaching would have to start at a very young age, all the way up to the late teens. After that, help will always be there for those who need it. No one would be forsaken.

This would be a very practical teaching, dealing with day-to-day issues as they arise, showing how to deal with them, and how to see and interact with those who think/act differently. Those who teach would be those who connect to some level of the truth being taught, and that live it. These are usually few in number, and those who display a propensity for such work should be nurtured early on. Without a strong foundation, no stable structure can be built. There would be no tests, no grades, no pass or fail, for life itself serves as the ultimate test. We would only strive to brew harmony through wisdom, love, and understanding in what are often very stormy waters.

This would not work as a private endeavor. It would have to be very much a part of the system, part of society. Otherwise, and despite all good intentions, the result would be more of the same.

I was truly happy. I had found a purpose and was well suited for it, but I ultimately had to recognize that I had no power to embark on such an undertaking. I nevertheless believe that such a thing will come to pass in the future, and why not? There is nothing to lose, really, and everything to gain.

Notwithstanding, I will not use this fact as an excuse to do nothing at all. As such, I will strive to help those who read this book and feel a need to connect. I will strive to help within reason, following some rules and guidelines. Remember that what's important has already been conveyed through this book, but if you feel a need to reach out, a form of contact will be given at the end of this book.

The roads of life are many and mysterious, but they are paved by our choices. I haven't spoken of it, but I could have chosen a different path. One filled with women and riches. Some outlined this "future" of possibilities, but I never longed for it. So instead, I chose to follow a different path. One of Consciousness. Was it the "right" choice? Many would consider it unfortunate, but yes, it was "right" for me.

In truth, one should not speak in terms of "right" or "wrong," for all choices are "right" in a sense. Some will see this statement as saying that there is no "right" or "wrong," which is not true. All readers will come in time to understand that these terms only make sense when considered in relation to a certain path.

The roads of life are indeed many and mysterious, but they will eventually lead to the very same place. We tend to judge choices based on the outcome, but such thinking is incorrect. There is no "wrong" or "right" in this. Only choices, and a branching out of possibility. Remember, knowing this fact does not discharge you from feeling the very real and inevitable consequences of any given choice. We all have our lessons to learn, and learn them, we must.

I've been given so much in this journey of life but had "failed" for so long to see it and understand it. Only now do I fully understand its nature and meaning. There have been many obstacles in this journey, but my greatest one was fear.

Fear and desire in their most basic, primal forms are quite natural to "worldly" living, but at times, it seems that this is the only language we speak and "understand." There is, of course, nothing wrong with living a worldly life. The real issue here arises when fear and desire drive us to disregard or act negatively toward another.

Fear can obstruct spiritual and material life. Those who fear material predicaments might find that bravery is enough to overcome most, but this is not enough for those who follow a spiritual road. Courage may help up to a point, but most will eventually realize that one has to go beyond fear itself.

The following parts of this book are very much a part of my journey, as was the tale of my life. They portray things that aided me in overcoming many obstacles, some more persistent than others. As such, I hope they serve to help you in a journey of your own, spiritual, material, or both.

The Life and Spiritual Journey of No One

PART TWO

The Spiritual Diet

The Life and Spiritual Journey of No One

Introduction

The more I dwell on the spiritual life, the more I see it as a nutritional diet. Generalizations can be made in either one, but each individual is unique and should be approached in a personalized way by the master or healer. No one diet fits all. There have to be different approaches or tweaks to a particular method. We all have very distinct levels of development—different minds, baggage (karma, desires, dysfunctions), physical conditions, and disabilities that prevent an individual from doing a particular thing or practicing in a certain way.

In the world of nutrition and fitness, there are difficult situations that make one think that it's hopeless or that "this is as far as I can go," but I know this is not true. It may be difficult to diagnose the problem(s) correctly or to find the proper method(s) to use. Still, I know for sure that everyone can be helped and taken well beyond what they thought possible.

In the world of fitness/nutrition, the professional has to have great insight, perception, experience, and various tools to guide and help others overcome obstacles. Following this path has shown me that the challenges can become exponentially more difficult. Understanding these facts has led me to write about certain subjects/practices that have come to help me and might come to help you.

The Life and Spiritual Journey of No One

Chapter One

Sex

This is a sensitive subject, and I will try to tread carefully. Religionists and spiritualists are often reluctant to touch on the subject. They usually offer vague answers, putting us in limbo or with even more questions, much like politicians. Most scripture dwells little on the subject but often warns about lustful desires that bring about evil and the fall of men. The lack of content on the topic is somewhat understandable. If such references were to be found in scripture, they would most probably be misunderstood and manipulated to serve one's own selfish desires, giving them, as it were, a free pass to do whatever they like.

As one on the spiritual path, I feel there is a real need to touch on the subject, even if just mildly, for if you are not an ascetic/monastic, questions, doubts, and fears will arise as you travel this road, as they did in me. I abstained from intimacy for more than ten months out of doubt. I even refrained from touching my wife, which is forced, not good, or natural.

The sexual impulse is no "sin," for it was given by Mother Nature and serves a purpose. The sexual impulse is nothing more than energy. In animals, sex is a need that drives them to copulate. Offspring are just a natural consequence of the release of that energy. In the animal kingdom, this energy is triggered and controlled by Mother Nature, but in man, things are different.

Here, the mind becomes the more prominent controller of the sex impulse (energy), making sex much more of a want than a need. In the animal kingdom, the word "desire" does not apply, for it is not pleasure that drives them, only the need for release.

We're not animals, and as such, we should refrain from acting like them. On the other hand, animals do not do what we do to each other. This exposition is not meant to address distortions of a sexual nature. They are numerous, and it is difficult and dangerous to just vaguely speak of them. Notwithstanding, I would like to say this: Be mindful of your roles in life. Do not misplace your sexual endeavors with those you should care for and protect. Do not abuse your position, given by age, blood, power, or rank. There is a right time to engage in such things, and puberty is often the driving force that triggers the curiosity of many. Physical intimacy should be informed and consensual. Proper education/understanding will go a long way in avoiding trouble, along with many forms of trauma that often last for a lifetime.

Scripture is often ill-interpreted as saying that one should not desire his own wife, but how can this be? Lust can indeed be an obstruction to material and spiritual life, but a "natural" sexual desire is very much a part of our human existence. So, the question comes to mind:

How does one know that it is lust one feels and not a natural sexual desire?

It may seem self-evident, but at times it may be hard to tell the difference. The best way is to analyze yourself:

- Do you often dwell in thoughts of a sexual nature?
- Do you dwell on them every day?
- Are your actions guided by this desire?
- Does it sprout jealousy?
- Does it give way to moods and anger?
- Do you desire others than your own?

- Do you indulge often?

These are a few examples, and they may appear impossible to overcome as they seem an established second nature, but I assure you they are not. A natural follow-up question would be: **How often Is too often?**

To answer this, there should be some understanding of the natures of men and women. The vital force required to create the conditions necessary for the generation of new life is high and of some influence in the spiritual practice, especially in the beginning. However, due to the different nature of the reproductive organs, this can come to affect men more than women. Women have their period scheduled for a particular time of the month, and men can produce sperm every time they indulge in sexual activity. Ergo, the potential loss of vital force is greater in men. This is not a free pass for women, for they face the same temptations and troubles as men.

Single people should at least abstain from mindlessly using others as vehicles for release. Such practices often end up doing harm to both parties. You should also realize that that drive will usually subside or completely disappear after your spiritual practice. However, the sexual energy may come to overwhelm many whether they are on the spiritual path or not. As such, masturbation might be a way to harmlessly release what seems impossible to control. Yes, I said "masturbation," it's not a bad word, and the act constitutes no "sin."

For those who have a significant other, love has its natural physical expression, holding its rightful place in every couple's life. Now I want to caution you about something. Some of you will interpret what I said as meaning that married couples should only resort to intimacy to bring children into the world, which is not the case. Along with free will, God has empowered you with reason and discrimination. Use them. Children are a great responsibility, so make sure you can properly raise and care for them. Again, to clarify, physical intimacy can be a natural and beautiful expression in the life of couples, even without the aim or thought of bearing children.

So how often is too often? If you indulge yourself almost every day, you can be sure that you are indulging too much. Other than that, it really doesn't matter. Everyone has a different starting point, as we are all different expressions of the same. Now I know there are those of you that will not be satisfied with anything but a number, and I could certainly provide you with one. Still, if I were to do so, one of two things would happen: You would either feel a sense of inadequacy for being unable to live up to it, or you'd become mechanical, obsessed in your attempts to comply, which would ultimately bind you to this process. Neither one is "good." So, lift this weight from your shoulders, realize the truth behind these words, and let go. No one else can do it for you.

On the other hand, focusing on how much is too much keeps you from realizing the more central obstruction in your path, which is the "mindset" you are in when you engage in sexual intimacy with others. Sexual energy may come to bring us together, but it's our minds that determine how we think/act. This obstruction will come to express itself literally, for it affects the flow of energy in our centers (chakras). This will happen if one is set on using others as a means for release, as instruments for one's own pleasure. The desire to control or to be controlled will also hinder your process, and so will fear.

It may seem that I'm painting a bleak picture of sexuality, but this is not my intent. Physical/sexual expression is truly a gift and can be a wonderful thing. The Tantric tradition speaks of this to some degree, and without knowing it, I've been living it ever since I decided to live a simpler life. In this world, we often have an inability to truly connect with each other, which leaves us both unsatisfied and conformed at the same time. After leaving my job and starting on a simpler path, my wife and I began to think differently, opening up, giving, loving, and understanding each other. Connecting on a deeper level through our hearts. This made our sexual experiences incredibly intense, deep, and fulfilling. It almost always ended in a very synchronized climax, but this wasn't at all the most gratifying part. We were "happy" and content.

The ways of love and understanding are the ways of the heart (chakra), the way we express and connect with others. This is just one of its forms of expression. I also came to realize that physical intimacy can also be experienced through the higher centers in our bodies. This came to me in my awakened state, and despite not being able to identify the chakra in question, I can say that this was a most profound, liberating experience. Without knowing anything about these things, I experienced them all. Still, at a certain point, I started to become judgmental, thinking that the ways of the spiritual abide only in celibacy/renunciation, which of course, is not true. Now I know better, and I hope you come to this understanding too. There is nothing wrong with either path, it's all just a matter of choice, and whatever that choice may be, you will find that, in time, you will come to outgrow these forms of expression.

Some of you may also inquire about other sexual orientations: **Are they natural? Why do they exist? Do they obstruct us from moving forward?** Any sexual orientation that strays from the norm is usually labeled as unnatural, which in itself bears the weight of judgment and little understanding. One should always strive to develop good judgment without the weight of being judgmental, for these are two very different things.

Many of us have been coming to this plane of existence for quite some time. We've reincarnated again and again into both male and female forms, which over time tends to create a bias that is brought into the world regardless of form (male/female). This fact can come to express itself in different ways. One of those is an incredible feeling of discomfort associated with seeing oneself in a particular type of body. With regards to obstruction, the simple answer is no. In essence, what obstructs is the same for all.

The Life and Spiritual Journey of No One

Chapter Two

Exercise

I have been exercising most of my life, and in a pretty serious way, but upon starting on this path, I began to be unsure about what to do, and my afflictions didn't make it any easier. The thing is that I didn't have any baseline to work with, so as a man of science, this made things very difficult. I tried different types of exercise, different intensities, training less and training lighter, but nothing seemed to help.

The first thing of crucial importance is body consciousness. Putting apart my ordeals, I was extremely body conscious. I could tell in fine detail what muscles were working in any given movement. As such, I had highly developed and sensitive motor nerves, which translated to an outspread of life force not conducive to spiritual practice. This is not a linear thing. Let's take squats, for instance. Over time less than perfect execution will cause muscles to cement in a certain way, causing issues with spinal alignment (sitting and upright).

Posture-related afflictions have become commonplace in western society. Some may come to affect life more than others, but everything related to the spine is a red flag. Impairments in the flow of life force in your spine will have very factual physical and spiritual repercussions, so avoiding detrimental forms of work is critical.

I'm not saying one in this particular path should not exercise, but a series of factors should be considered. Exercises that exert stress on the heart and body are to be avoided, hatha yoga and other oriental practices might be good alternatives, but the elasticity of the muscle and tendons is a factor to be considered before undertaking some of these practices. For your understanding, I will describe a fairly normal yogic state of being: In a rested state, the average person takes five to ten breaths in the amount of time needed for the yogi to take one. This fact leads to a slower heartbeat in yogis, which reflects itself in the individual's life span. Animals are different life forms, but you can take them as an example. Those with lower heart rates (ex: Elephant - 30 b/min ⇨ 65 Years) live longer than those with high (ex: Rats - 380 b/min ⇨ 2 Years).

After a while of trying to figure things out, I decided to stop exercising, and in three weeks, I started seeing improvements in my practice. My body consciousness started to subside and continued to do so. Now I walk. You might inquire about bike riding. Well, I do that too, just not as much. If you live in the Netherlands or in any such place with similar conditions, I would say that bike riding would be a great form of exercise, but I should refrain from making generalizations. We live in a world where variety/diversity prevail. So just try to find what's best for you.

Finding Middle Ground

Throughout most of my life, I have been focused on the material aspects of my existence, which has taken its toll. However, I have come to realize that solely focusing on the spiritual aspects of life can also come at a price. After four years of minimal exercise, I discovered that leaning too heavily towards one side is not beneficial at all. My body had become frail, gained fat in all the wrong places, and lacked greatly in glycogen reserves. My joints, posture, and metabolic flexibility were all affected. The consequences of physical inactivity tend to worsen over time. So, after careful consideration, I decided to take action and incorporate exercise into my routine. Starting from scratch provided me with the perfect baseline.

To begin, I adopted a slow and measured approach, focusing mainly on functional training and some specific muscle work. My aim was to derive maximum benefit from my workouts, and functional training seemed like the ideal method to achieve this. My training sessions encompass a variety of exercises targeting muscular development, posture, flexibility, and fat burning. Although it may seem unusual to some, it is indeed possible to efficiently address all of these aspects within a single session.

After just a few training sessions, I noticed significant improvements both outwardly and inwardly. Surprisingly, my cardiovascular capacity was already in good shape, which I attribute to the breath work involved in my spiritual practice. This newfound middle ground not only enhanced my health and well-being but also deepened my connection to the Infinite. From the very beginning, I experienced a profound increase in Light and Awareness. This newfound balance has become part of the foundation upon which I continue to improve.

This form of training is suitable and adaptable for individuals of all ages, but each one has to make their own choice and find their own balance. However, I would like to highlight a few points that everyone should consider.

Important Factors:

1. **Cost/Benefit**: What is the cost of doing or not doing something? What is the benefit? Cost/benefit is something to consider in almost all aspects of life. Mindful fitness professionals apply this principle when designing training sessions and exercises tailored to the individual. I always strive to derive the most benefit from my workouts, but this requires experience and know-how. For most people this will take some time to figure out.

2. **Intensity**: I avoid high-intensity training that places excessive stress on the heart and body. While a certain level of effort is necessary for training or exercise to be effective, I focus mostly on building up what is good, rather than destroying it. It's also important to remember that what is high intensity for some might not be for others, so exercising good judgment is crucial.

3. **Frequency**: For most individuals, training two to three times a week is essential. The duration of each session should range from 50 to 75 minutes, depending on the individual, their goals, and the chosen training method. Scheduling and spacing out sessions should be based on factors such as recovery, nutrition, sleep, and fasting, so be sure to consider these aspects before starting.

We are spiritual beings living a physical existence, whether we acknowledge it or not. While a quiet state of being should be our norm, engaging in properly planned and controlled forms of exercise can and will contribute to a more balanced existence with oneself and the world. Therefore, I encourage you to discover what fits into your own balanced way of living.

Chapter Three

Food

Now food and nutrition are definitely part of my field. I've dwelled and worked with them for many years, but I never considered being a vegetarian. Of course, now things were different, and I was willing to change. I just didn't know the best way to do it until I went to India. Surely this was the best way, and many thousands of years of experience can attest to that. I just couldn't reproduce it at home. One must adjust to their circumstances and make the best out of them.

You may be faced with issues regarding allergies or intolerances (e.g., dairy) to some types of food, which sometimes complicates things in an already restrictive diet. These, with some work, can be overcome to some extent, but not always. You should also realize that every new diet has its own acclimatization period. There are so many things one could say about such a subject that a whole book could be written about it, and many have been, but if you don't have any issues, the best way to go about it is to keep it simple and varied, and if you can, go organic.

On another level, I can say that pure foods have a positive effect on your life and practice. Vegetables and fruits are the highest-ranked, but the latter surpasses all others by far, and I have confirmed it to be so through my center (spiritual eye). Fruits are the most spiritual foods, and most can be eaten without "taint"; it's like they were created with such an intent. You have but to understand the natural order of things.

Eating, as a general rule, implies taking life. Animals carry no obstruction, for they are driven by the instincts they've been given, but such is not the case for men. The more complex the life form one eats, the bigger the strain, the obstruction one bestows on oneself. The exception to this would be fruit. Dairy products may also fall into this category, although men have distorted their natural flow in life.

When you consume fruit, there is no obstruction, for it does not imply the death of the one that bears it. The seeds, carriers of new life, are often indigestible and rarely eaten. One just ends up contributing to the cycle of life.

Now, with that said, I don't believe there are many "souls" that can survive on vegetables and fruits alone. Some starchy carbs and protein are needed. The human body doesn't require enormous amounts of protein, but it needs some, which one can easily get from their diet if they're not striving to become a vegan. The following table presents protein sources available in a vegetarian diet. Still, you must realize that not all proteins are created equal; they vary in biological value, and those of animal origin are always of the highest grade. Proteins from vegetable sources are often not as bioavailable or complete. They are prone to contain antinutritional factors that prevent the absorption of nutrients (protein - amino acids in this case).

Table 1º - Protein content in foods suitable for vegetarians.

Sources	Food	% of Protein
Animal (for vegetarians)	Eggs	12,6
	Cheese (Cow)	25
	Greek Yogurt (Cow)	10
	Natural Yogurt (Cow)	3,4
	Milk (Cow)	3,4
Vegetable	Soybeans*	36
	Soybeans sprouts	13,1
	Lentils	9,0
	Beans** (on average)	8,5
	Chickpeas	8,3
	Lime beans	6,8
	Peas	5,4
	Quinoa	4,4
	Mushrooms	3,6
	Spinach	3,0
Nuts & Seeds	Hemp seeds	31,6
	Pumpkin seeds	29,8
	Peanuts	24,4
	Almonds	21,2
	Pistachio	21,1
	Sunflower seeds	19,3
	Flax seeds	18,3
Fruits	Guavas	2,6
	Avocados	2,0
	Apricots	1,4

Note – Source: The U.S. Department of Agriculture.
* - I use Soybeans as a reference because they represent soy in its richest nutritional form.
** - Beans tend to cause gastric disorders (flatulence), which are things to be avoided. However, different people will have different sensibilities, which is something to keep in mind while arranging your diet.

The examples given in Table 1 are just a few options from which you can build your diet, but I'm well aware that some are easier to fit and use than others, primarily due to the individual and their unique circumstances. It's important to note that the body has the ability to recycle protein and reuse it whenever it deems necessary. This process becomes increasingly more efficient as you start engaging in the practice of fasting.

One should also eat enough starchy carbs to sustain their body and activity, whatever it may be. Rice, potatoes, sweet potatoes, and bread are my foods of choice. Yes, I said bread. I don't see the issue here, although I'm often surprised to see what passes for bread these days. If you live in a place/country where quality bread is easy to come by, why not take advantage of it**?** I used to eat oatmeal, but it didn't seem to fit so well with this diet. That might not be the case for you. This diet puts little emphasis on fats, so limit yourself to moderate use of them. Strive to use healthy fats, preferably of vegetable origin. The only exceptions I make are for butter and ghee.

The number of meals a day is also an essential factor. As you meditate and advance, your metabolism slows down. On the other hand, eating too soon before practice may hinder the practitioner. Advice is usually given to wait at least three hours before Kriya practice. If you eat six times a day, you can easily strive for four meals a day and, after a while, work down to three, which is the norm in the ashrams in India. This is not my usual routine. I usually engage in a particular form of fasting, which I will explain in the following chapter.

Key Nutrients - Sources

There are different forms of vegetarianism, and whatever one you lean toward, you should realize that some nutritional deficiencies might arise. Depending on which form one consciously or unconsciously follows, deficiencies may develop over time, namely iron, calcium, zinc, omega-3, vitamin D, B2, B12, and iodine. I'm not criticizing any particular diet one chooses to embark on. I'm just trying to raise awareness and understanding of how the lack of these nutrients may affect your body and, ultimately, your health.

The following table displays dietary requirements along with appropriate food sources for these key nutrients. However, it bears to be mentioned that vitamin D3 (cholecalciferol) can be synthesized in the skin via UVB radiation. A good blood level of vitamin D can be attained through regular 15 to 30 minutes of sunlight exposure with a UV index of three or more. The time of day one should do so may vary due to location and season, and it is unwise for me to give general guidelines. One should also consider skin tone in the equation; darker-skinned individuals will need longer exposure periods to produce the same amounts of vitamin D. Nowadays, online services allow you to check UV levels for any particular time or place worldwide.

Table 2º - Key nutrients on a plant-based diet, Recommended Dietary Allowances, food sources, and nutritional amount.

Nutrient		RDA*			Food	Portion	[ ]
Iron	Age	11-18	19-50	51+	Dark chocolate	100 g	8.13 mg
					Cooked Soybeans	100 g	4.79 mg
	Male	11 mg	8 mg	8 mg	Boiled spinach	100 g	3.57 mg
					Boiled lentils	100 g	3.3 mg
					Chickpeas	100 g	2.9 mg
					Pumpkin seeds	28 g	2.25 mg
	Female	15 mg	18 mg	8 mg	Canned Kidney beans	100 g	2.08 mg
					Cooked quinoa	100 g	1.49 mg
					Cooked broccoli	100 g	1.2 mg
Calcium	Age	14-18	19-50	51-70	Cheddar cheese	100 g	707 mg
					Blackstrap molasses	2 Tbsp	400 mg
	Male	1300 mg	1000 mg	1000 mg	Soy yogurt	100 g	206 mg
					Soy milk	100 g	155 mg
	Female	1300 mg	1000 mg	1200 mg	Whole milk yogurt	100 g	121 mg
					Whole milk	100 g	119 mg
Zinc	Age	8-13	14-18	19+	Cheddar cheese	100 g	3.65 mg
	Male	8 mg	11 mg	11 mg	Pumpkin seeds	28 g	2.17 mg
					Cashew butter	28 g	1.46 mg
					Boiled lentils	100 g	1.27 mg
	Female	8 mg	9 mg	9 mg	Brewer's yeast	1 Tbsp	0.95 mg
					Peanut butter	28 g	0.85 mg
Vitamin D	Age	1-70	70+		Eggs	100 g	5.45 µg
	Male	15 µg	20 µg		Whole milk	100 g	1.1 µg
	Female	15 µg	20 µg		Whole milk yogurt	100 g	0.78 µg
Vitamin B$_2$	Age	14-18	19+		Brewer's yeast	30 g	5.49 mg
	Male	1.3 mg	1.3 mg		Whole milk yogurt	245 g	0.9 mg
					Cheddar cheese	100 g	0.44 mg
	Female	1.0 mg	1.1 mg		Eggs	1 large	0.2 mg
Vitamin B$_{12}$	Age	9-13	14+		Whole milk	244 g	0.88 µg
	Male	1.8 µg	2.4 µg		Whole Greek yogurt	100 g	0.75 µg
					Whole milk yogurt	125 g	0.6 µg
	Female	1.8 µg	2.4 µg		Eggs	1 large	0.51 µg
Omega 3's	Age	9-13	14+		Flax seed oil	1 Tbsp	7.26 g
	Male	1.2 g	1.6 g		Ground chia seeds	28 g	5.06 g
					Walnuts	28 g	2.57 g
	Female	1.0 g	1.1 g		Flax seeds	1 Tbsp	2.35 g
					Canola oil	1 Tbsp	1.28 g
Iodine	Age	9-13	14+		Dried nori seaweed	5 g	116 µg
	Male	120 µg	150 µg		Nonfat Greek yogurt	185 g	0.87 µg
					Nonfat milk	244 g	0.85 µg
	Female	120 µg	150 µg		Whole milk yogurt	125 g	0.6 µg

Note – Source: The U.S. Department of Agriculture.
* - Source: National Institute of Health, Office of Dietary Supplements, USA.

As you can attest yourself, most of these products have a limited amount of these nutrients in their composition. So, you have to consider how much quantity and variety you can fit into your meals, and if you fast a lot, this problem becomes even more significant. Thus, one should always have some sort of plan, but in certain cases, the intake of nutritional supplements might be almost unavoidable. I suggest preparing vegetables, veggie burgers, and other recipes with brewer's yeast. Aside from providing great taste to whatever is eaten (cooked or raw), it will supply your body with important minerals like phosphorus, magnesium, zinc, and chromium, along with a hefty dose of vitamins B1, B2, and B3. Still, all other nutrients will have to be addressed separately. Iodine, for example, may become a challenge for many, but resorting to iodized salt as part of a more global approach may help achieve nutritional quotas.

One should always try to have an all-rounded diet that includes all the necessary nutrients for one's body. However, at times, this might not be an easy endeavor for several reasons. So, try to create strategies that suit you and come naturally to you, or you'll inadvertently deviate and fall into one or more nutritional deficiencies.

You should also be mindful of the way you prepare food. Cooking, as you may know, improves digestion and absorption of many nutrients. However, some cooking methods significantly reduce the content of several key nutrients in your food due to temperature and/or process. For instance, vitamins C and B are water-soluble and heat-sensitive nutrients, so one should avoid boiling and/or overheating foods containing such nutrients. This applies to minerals as well, and certain processes may drain foods of minerals like potassium, magnesium, sodium, and calcium.

I will not go into much detail on this, but try to cook your vegetables for only a few minutes whenever possible. Eat them within a day of cooking them. Don't peel your vegetables if you don't have to, and avoid boiling them. However, if you must boil them, use the resulting water to make soup.

Deficiencies and Symptoms

Table 3° - Symptoms of nutrient deficiencies.

Nutrient Deficiency	Symptoms
Iron	Fatigue (weakness), lightheadedness, confusion, loss of concentration, sensitivity to cold, shortness of breath, rapid heartbeat, pale skin, hair loss, brittle nails, and pica: cravings for dirt, clay, ice, or other non-food items.
Calcium	Muscle cramps or weakness. Numbness or tingling in fingers. Abnormal heart rate and poor appetite. Continued calcium deficiency will lead firstly to osteopenia and, if untreated, osteoporosis.
Zinc	Loss of taste or smell. Poor appetite, depressed mood, decreased immunity, delayed wound healing, delayed sexual maturation, hypogonadism, diarrhea, and hair loss.
Vitamin D	Getting sick often, prone to infection, fatigue/tiredness, bone and back pain, depression, impaired wound healing, bone loss, hair loss, and muscle pain.
Vitamin B_2	Cracked lips, sore throat, swelling of the mouth and throat, swollen tongue (glossitis), hair loss, skin rash, anemia, Itchy red eyes, and cataracts in severe cases
Vitamin B_{12}	Megaloblastic anemia, Pernicious anemia, fatigue (weakness), Nerve damage with numbness, and tingling in the hands and legs. Memory loss, confusion, dementia, depression, and seizures.
Omega 3's	Dry skin, brittle nails, chicken skin, dermatitis, dandruff, dry eyes, attention/concentration problems, irritability, joint discomfort, fatigue, and poor sleep quality.
Iodine	Fatigue, lethargy, weakness, sensitivity to cold, constipation, dry skin and hair, and weight gain.

Note – Sources: National Institute of Health, Office of Dietary Supplements, USA. Harvard T.H. Chan, School of Public Health: The Nutrition Source.

Table 3 depicts the various symptoms associated with the lack of the above-mentioned nutrients. As you can see, many of these symptoms are non-specific and may be associated with other health conditions. Therefore, a specific deficiency may be wrongly addressed and/or go unnoticed for quite some time, so a more in-depth analysis may be required to determine the nutrient at fault. It's also important to note that overcoming certain nutrient deficiencies will take some time and work to resolve. For example, a deficiency in vitamin D will take up to six to eight weeks to overcome, even with the proper supplementation. Iron is another curious example: calcium, certain teas, coffee, and other caffeinated drinks reduce iron absorption, while vitamin C promotes it. Thus, overcoming an iron deficiency will require time, work, and planning, even when taking supplements.

With that said, I would like to state that in a balanced vegetarian diet, our bodies tend, over time, to become increasingly more efficient in absorbing, recycling, and synthesizing the nutrients they need. As such, nutritional deficiencies are not as common as you might think.

The Life and Spiritual Journey of No One

Chapter Four

Fasting

I had some fasting experience before starting on this path — like I was preparing for it somehow. Upon arriving back from India, I started fasting regularly, sometimes twice a week, but normally once. I always perceived purer, cleaner energy while fasting but also experienced great difficulty in practice. I was unable to draw in life air or sustain posture. I would feel faint, and cold sweat would come over me — so much so that I would have to lie down on the floor. Despite all these difficulties, I continued for a long time , following to the letter what I was given. After Kriya's initiation, things improved slightly, but I still felt it wasn't helping.

The scientific community has been directing its attention more and more to fasting. It has come to recognize, by way of scientific proof, the value of such ancient wisdom. Fasting directs your body to use cleaner sources of energy. It also brings about many health benefits such as reduced inflammation, fat loss, a boosted immune system, and autophagy, among others. However, fasting is not just for the benefit of the body but also for the mind and spirit. Fasting has been a well-known spiritual practice for those who walk the path long before any scientific recognition of its effects on the body. Physically, I could handle fasting just fine, but I didn't seem to be getting the spiritual benefit from it.

There are many forms of fasting, and I'm not going to dwell on them all. Like in so many things, there is no one-size-fits-all solution. There are limiting factors, such as medical conditions, age, metabolic rate, body type, and even spiritual development. What worked for me — and might work for you — is a form of intermittent fasting, which is basically a time-restrictive eating window within a day (24 hours).

There are three types:

20/4 protocol - Here, you have a four-hour eating window followed by twenty hours of fasting. Generally, you can eat to your heart's satisfaction during the four-hour feasting window, but I advise against it. If you do so, you'll just be delaying the digestive process, limiting the number of calories and nutrients you can take in during such a short time, and it's just not healthy to do so. Just strive to place your meals at the beginning and end of your eating window. This form of fasting generally works better and is easier to handle for those over the age of 35-40.

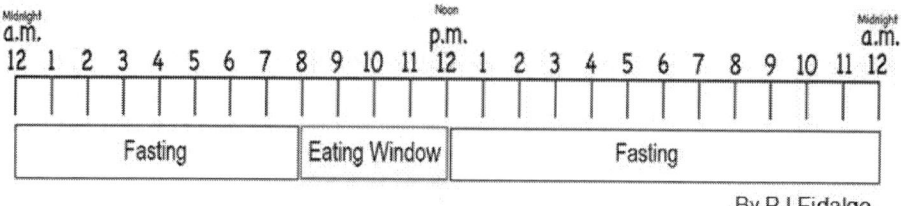

Diagram 1º - The 20/4 intermittent fasting.

18/6 protocol - Here, you have a six-hour eating window followed by eighteen hours of fasting. This eating window is simpler to work with because it's easier to fit your meals/food and simultaneously allow for their proper digestion. I would advise making only two meals, if you can, at the beginning and end of your eating window. If you cannot handle this, you can snack in between. This form of fasting generally works better and is easier to handle for those under the age of 35-40.

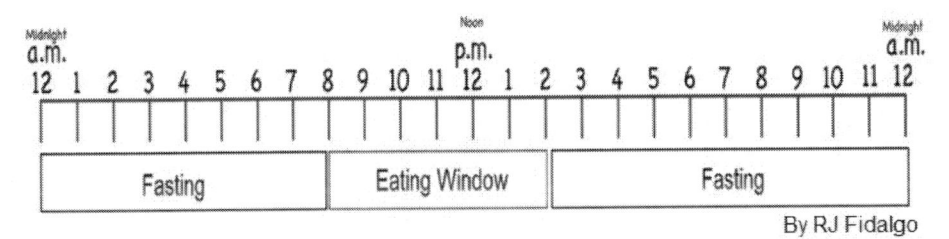

Diagram 2º - The 18/6 intermittent fasting.

16/8 protocol - Here, you have an eight-hour eating window followed by sixteen hours of fasting. This eating window may be easier physically, but for those who practice meditation, especially yogic breathing techniques, it becomes harder to work with, and I will explain why later. This eating window fits three meals easily, which should be evenly spaced in time and calories. Alternatively, your second meal can be lighter than the others, or you might choose to have only two meals. Much like the previous form of fasting, the 16/8 tends to be easier and works better for those under the age of 35-40.

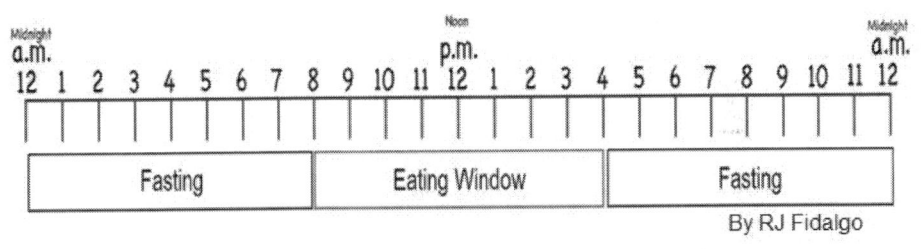

Diagram 3º - The 16/8 intermittent fasting.

Remember, if you make your regular three meals — breakfast, lunch, and dinner — you can easily strive to do one of these. Otherwise, try to decrease the number of meals gradually. Like I said before, ease your body into it.

Now, for one engaged in meditation, there are some things to consider before starting or choosing a fasting routine: how many hours do you sleep; how many times do you practice meditation, how long, and at what time; do you use more "strenuous" forms of breathing in your practice ; what's your work schedule ; time preparing and cooking meals ; can you easily fit meals during the day, or do you have a fixed schedule for it, etc.

You can do these routines every day or choose to do them a few days a week or most days of the week. Be sure to know that there are benefits to doing them every single day. Another question that might or might not be on your mind is whether you can change these eating windows . Of course, you can. You can choose to do a 5-hour eating window (19/5) or a 7-hour eating window (17/7). Such things are not set in stone, and sometimes an hour makes all the difference. This knowledge does not belong to any one person. It's very, very ancient wisdom. Ramadan is an excellent example of that knowledge put into practice without being overly technical.

Sometimes — well, most of the time — it becomes quite difficult for a family man or woman to juggle all these things together and make them work. There are only so many hours in a day, but this tool might make your life and practice a little easier. You can move these eating windows to best fit your needs and lifestyle, but as you can now understand, some are easier to work with than others. Of course, not every day will fit perfectly with your routine, and that's OK. Just do your best.

Chapter Five

Ekadashi and Fasting

Ekadashi may be familiar to some but strange to most, especially to Westerners. This term refers to the eleventh lunar day of each of the two lunar phases that occur in a lunar month, and it has everything to do with fasting. For a very long time, I found no particular spiritual benefit to 24-hour fasts — much less to even more extended periods (48-72 hours). Most of the time, it felt like I was taking a step back, not forward, but that changed when I found Ekadashi. As it turns out, there seems to be a day when our whole being (body, mind, and spirit) displays the best predisposition to reap the most benefits out of fasting. The flow of energy feels different in quality and intensity. At times, I felt it more on a previous or subsequent day. Curiously enough, the days surrounding Ekadashi are said to be equally important, and some say that one should fast for the whole three-day period.

Now, I'm not an advocate of this practice. However, the best day to engage in fasting may differ from individual to individual, and it might be one of these three: the 10th - Dashami, the 11th - Ekadashi, or the 12th - Dwadashi.

It is said that one should always fast on Ekadashi or at least partially in accordance with one's ability to do so. For example, one could do a liquid fast (milk, juice), eat only fruits, or fruits and vegetables, while always refraining from eating grains. Still, it should be stated that the spiritual benefit derived from such practices diminishes as we move further down the ladder.

Now, saying that one should fast on this particular day is an oversimplification. There are twenty-four Ekadashi in a lunar calendar (twenty-six in a leap year), and many have specific observances attached to them. But other than always thinking and praising the Lord in one way or another, there appear to be only three common denominators to all Ekadashi's: no eating, no drinking, and no sleeping for 24 hours.

Physically speaking, one day of dry fasting (no foods or liquids) provides the same benefits as 3 days of overall fasting. Now, I cannot say how this relates to the mental and spiritual aspects of our being, but I can surely say that this practice has true value on Ekadashi. The reasoning behind not sleeping is a little trickier, but there seems to be a difference between 24 hours of active fasting versus passively fasting part of the time (in sleep).

All I could say for certain at first was that there is a loss of conscious focus while one sleeps, but that was it. After engaging in this practice, I can now say that it has a substantial spiritual benefit — but it does take its toll, which does not seem to diminish all that much with experience.

Now you might ask: **"Should I do it?"** I don't know. Only you can really answer that question. The only thing I can do is relay my perceptions and convey some practical advice.

Guidelines:

- ➢ Ease yourself into regular water fasting (24 hours), which I've talked about to some extent in the previous chapter.

- ➢ If you are already able to fast normally, try performing your fasts on Ekadashi.

- ➢ After gaining some experience with fasting, try dry fasting once in a while.

- ➢ Become proficient at dry fasting. Some individuals will have an easier time with this than others due to various factors. Take your time.

➢ Once you become proficient at dry fasting, pick an auspicious day (Ekadashi) to do 24 hours of active dry fasting (no sleep):

- You will feel some weariness on the following day.

- You will most likely tend to oversleep the following morning.

Plan your sleepless nights:

- The hours will seem to drag out if you're doing nothing.

- Focusing on work or doing chores around the house will not help. You can do some work, of course, but if you focus too much on this, you'll just be wasting your time, and you might as well be sleeping.

- Go for a night walk if you can.

- Engage in spiritual activity, watch a spiritual movie, listen to scripture or other spiritual work, meditate longer if you can, etc.

Be mindful that the Ekadashi in question might not be the right day for you. It might be that the best day for you is the 10th or the 12th and not the 11th (Ekadashi). In such a case, the benefit derived from not sleeping will be marginal at best. If you cultivate a certain degree of awareness, you might be able to perceive which day is right for you, making, in a way, your own calendar for fasting.

Remember — don't force anything. Doing so will only make an already hard path even harder. I have learned this lesson the hard way. I have made many mistakes. Fortunately, no irreparable damage was done, and I was able to get back on track.

I remember that one time I forced myself to meditate for ten hours. I thought that if I did, I might accomplish something, and I did — just not what I had expected. Pain and discomfort were my profit.

I recall that in the final moments of my trial, I couldn't even move. My muscles and joints were painfully cemented in place. Only through great effort was I able to move and rest on the floor.

Fasting and Infection

It is undeniably true that fasting boosts your immune system, but this is an overall truth that gives little insight into how the body goes about achieving this. My intent is not to overextend or be too scientific on the subject. However, raising awareness among those who engage in such practice is essential.

Prolonged fasts (24 hours or more) cause a crash of the immune system, which in turn signals the body to boost its defenses once the fast is broken. It is true that the immune system of some is stronger than others, but this crash makes the body of "anyone" more vulnerable to infection (virus/bacteria).

So, fasting (24 hours or more) might not be the best idea if you're already dealing with a pathogen in your body. You will have a particularly hard time dealing with new viruses. They will exact a heavier toll and take that much longer to recover from.

So how do you know that you're already dealing with an infection? Practically speaking, there are light symptoms that may hint at their presence, but if you are in close contact with infected hosts, in all likelihood, you already are. I am not trying to scare anyone. These are just facts of life. Just strive to deal with them wisely.

You should also be aware that more restrictive/conditioned forms of fasting take a more significant "toll" on your body, leaving it more vulnerable to foreign agents of decay. Personally, I engage in 24-hour fasts, which is the typical length of Ekadashi, but I strive not to be mechanical in my doing. If I'm unwell, I just don't do it. There are always more opportunities in the future.

Chapter Six

Gut Health

This is an important subject that involves food and fasting, eating and not eating. This seemingly insignificant subject has an enormous impact on your health, well-being, and spiritual practice. Before diving into the topic, I would like to address food intolerances and allergies — how they differ, and how one can be overcome while the other worsens over time.

Food allergies and intolerances often have similar symptoms. Because of this, they tend to be confused by many, but they differ in nature.

Food allergies are issues pertaining to the immune system. Certain foods have compounds (often proteins) that induce the body to produce high levels of antibodies as a defense, which translates into varied symptoms that range in severity but, in extreme cases, lead to death. People are commonly allergic to shellfish, nuts, fish, and eggs. Symptoms range from rash or hives to nausea, cramping, stomach pain, diarrhea, swelling, and shortness of breath. Usually, allergy-related symptoms worsen over time and not the other way around. There are exceptions, and children may experience milder symptoms as they come of age. Either way, it is important to note that whether allergies improve or worsen is completely out of one's control.

On the other hand, food intolerance stems from issues related to the digestive system, mainly in the gastrointestinal tract. Many substances can cause distress in the gut, but they are often caused by certain types of carbs and proteins. Some of the most well-known are lactose and gluten. Their intake usually leads to symptoms like nausea, diarrhea, bloating, cramps, and stomach pain.[22]

These intolerances have everything to do with gut health. As such, they can be addressed and overcome to a certain point, if not completely. Many state that intolerances tend to worsen over time, and although this might be true to a certain extent, it will only be so if you do nothing about it. Bear in mind that this discussion is not meant to address any particular intolerance but aims to achieve overall health and well-being through the gut.

The microorganisms present in the gut play a crucial role in digestive health, the immune system, and overall well-being. Your gut flora is predominantly made up of bacteria. They are vast in numbers (over 100 trillion) and belong to more than five hundred species. Every human has a core set of common microorganisms, but each person has a distinct and highly variable makeup of gut bacteria. Regardless of this fact, it is possible to fine-tune your gut bacteria to work for you and not against you.

There are mainly two factors that contribute to gut health: **food and fasting.**

Human studies have shown that the makeup of what we eat, both in terms of quality and quantity, can help modulate the composition and metabolic activity of the microbial communities in your gut. A healthy, balanced vegetarian diet is one such example. Another factor of greater and more immediate impact is when you eat. In other words, how long you go without eating (fasting or time-restricted feeding). Studies have revealed that fasting restores microbe diversity in the gut, increases tolerance against "bad" gut microbes, and restores the integrity of the intestinal epithelium.

---

[22] Do not mistake intolerance to gluten with celiac disease. They are two very different things. The latter is an immune disorder in which consuming gluten damages the lining of the small intestine. In that case, there is a definite need to consult a doctor or nutritionist about adopting a gluten-free diet.

By fasting, you can not only control the quality of the bacteria in your gut but also modulate their cycles of activity (circadian rhythm), gaining metabolic flexibility and reducing gut disorders, thus promoting good overall health and well-being. In simpler terms, through certain forms of fasting, we can control when the bacteria in our gut "eat" and "sleep," improving in turn our body's ability to transition from burning sugar to burning fat, and vice versa. These benefits translate into an overall positive effect on body and mind.

This is also one of the reasons I resort to intermittent fasting. This time-restricted feeding window allows you to regulate the cycle of activity (circadian rhythm) of the bacteria within your gut. This allows your life and spiritual practice to go unobstructed, as gastrointestinal disorders are all but over — or at least reduced to a minimum.

When you do a 24-hour fast once a week or a 48- or 72-hour fast once a month, the result is not the same. There is no question about the benefits of these forms of fasting, but regulating the cycles of activity of the bacteria within your gut is just not possible in this way. To regulate these cycles, it's important to be consistent. Changing hours, fasting intervals, and the number of meals will not produce the desired result.

This modulation of cycles is also possible with the One Meal a Day protocol (OMAD), but I do not endorse this form of eating/fasting as a lifestyle.

Probiotics - Kefir

As you can see, there seems to be a recurrent theme here, and you should realize that the only thing you can actually have some "control" over is your intake (its timing, nature, quantity, and quality). The rest will be as it will be. Your body will always act according to its program to the best of its ability at any given moment. On this note, the consumption of probiotic foods has been shown to significantly improve gut health. They are nothing more than beneficial microorganisms present in certain foods and dietary supplements that, when consumed, provide clear health benefits.

There are many probiotic foods, but I consider <u>homemade</u> Kefir to be the topmost. Its grains contain a large number of bacteria and yeast, making them a very rich and diverse probiotic that helps restore balance in your gut, offering protection against various types of harmful bacteria. It's not surprising to see good bacteria having a positive effect on your gut, but it may surprise you to learn that kefir can also act as an agent against cancer and dementia. Scientific studies have proven as much, but kefir intake should always be part of a more global approach that involves both food and fasting.

Kefir can and should be taken on a regular basis, but it's important to avoid taking too much. Many people assume that more is better, but this is rarely the case. If you eat three meals a day, two tablespoons per meal are more than enough, but if, for some reason, you are only able to take it once, three to four tablespoons will be a suitable measure.

As I said, there are many probiotic foods, and yogurt is likely the most widely known. Consuming kefir doesn't necessarily mean you have to exclude yogurt from your diet. Over the years, I have found that if I eat kefir on a regular basis and yogurt from time to time, I achieve the best possible result. However, this might not be true for you, so experiment and find what suits you best.

Conclusion

Don't be too mindful of trying to replicate what I do or of memorizing the specifics of any one routine. There is no secret to what I do, and I could certainly give a detailed description of it, but doing so would hold little value. Every individual is different in so many ways, and routines change. Mine has changed in many aspects, and it will continue to change in the future. Nothing ever stays the same in this world. Just make sure you are doing your best without forcing anything. Take what I've shared and create your own recipe. Change and adapt whenever you feel it's necessary. Don't be overly rigid or controlling. Such things will most surely hinder you. Be conscientious, and you'll find that whatever's unnecessary will eventually fall away.

The Life and Spiritual Journey of No One

PART THREE

Understanding

The Life and Spiritual Journey of No One

Introduction

The purpose of all true scripture is to aid in the evolution of man toward the One (God), and although their goal is the same, some are more comprehensive than others. As such, it must be said that the Hindu scriptures are in their highest form. I cannot say they are perfect, for perfection is not of this world, but they are arguably in their most "complete" form. Even if Truth were to be conveyed in its perfect form, it is bound to attain some level of taint from the one who receives it. Still, if somehow Truth manages to remain untouched in this process, it will surely not survive the influence of time, for all things that come into this world degrade, and are bound to disappear sooner or later. This principle holds true for both the spoken and written word.

In the western world, it is very hard to grasp these truths as they are conveyed through Hindu scripture, making the goal of their existence almost impossible to reach.

The following exposition is not meant to replace scripture. I aim only to clarify and present, in a comprehensive and simple manner, certain subjects that I feel might become obstacles in the realization of the One. As such, I advise you to read or hear the "Bhagavad Gita," "Mahabharata," and "Srimad Bhagavatam," written by Veda Vyasa, preferably in this order. May those who have already done so see things with new eyes, and may those who are yet to set their eyes or ears on such books do so with open hearts and minds.

On the other hand, I do not intend to create a following or a new path to enlightenment. That path has already been given by Paramahansa Yogananda and other great souls who came into this Earth to help others. I am but an instrument that strives, by the grace of God, to untangle the knots of misconceptions that may hinder our lives and our process of connecting.

Early on in my spiritual path, I was told that I already knew the answers I was seeking and that I was free to dismiss any teaching that didn't sit right with me. This, of course, left me puzzled for quite some time. However, this truth came to reveal itself in many ways and forms. Ultimately, it led to what is written in this section and on the road of my life. Bear in mind that I did not dismiss anything of my own conscious accord. In fact, I had a pretty hard time doing so, but the truth is that many teachings left me uneasy within, which, in turn, placed me at a standstill, whether I was conscious of it or not. Only the realization of the undistorted truth opened the spiritual road ahead, and this can and will happen to you too.[23]

---

[23] For a long time, the idea of such divine souls speaking in "error" or giving imperfect truths was inconceivable to me. Bear in mind that this was never their "intention." This is the product of a very much-needed Universal Law, which in turn leads Truth to be distorted to a greater or lesser degree. In some cases, what is given is not an "error" per se, just a part of a much larger truth or a very particular point of view. Notwithstanding, these forms of exposition can at times hinder more than they help. I know that many of you will have a hard time accepting this, just like I did, but there are inevitably things that obstruct you, and if you don't keep an open mind and an open heart, they will undoubtedly continue to do so, hindering you on the road to travel.

Chapter One

God and The Spiritual World

God is One, ever-existing, ever-conscious, ever-new bliss. In Hinduism, He is called Krishna, but this is not a widely accepted concept even for Hindus. Some see Him as just another avatar (avatāra) of the primal consciousness in creation—Vishnu, no more important than any other.

My original intent was to make a clear and simplified exposition of the word avatar, but I found it to be impossible. Many translate the word to mean incarnation, but this is such a restrictive word that it could never equate to the original Sanskrit word avatāra. There are, in fact, no English words—or combinations of them—that can equate to the original. There is true value in understanding the meaning behind the word, but I failed to properly convey it. Just bear in mind that the word was originally meant to refer to higher consciousness and that there are various grades of it, including the Original One.

Some will come to accept Krishna, while others will have a hard time granting or accepting a name or form to what they consider unfathomable. I believe that saying that Krishna is the most complete "form" (Consciousness) of the Lord to have ever come to this plane of existence might just be the safest and most proper statement to make. Nonetheless, seeing Krishna as the Original One will help shed light on the flow of the Spiritual to the Material.

Many strive to know God through His impersonal features, while others seek Him on a more personal level. This has been the subject of discord since time immemorial, but I say that one does not exclude the other. Before continuing, I would like to say this: Names and forms can hold power, but they are subjective nonetheless. I say this because God has been given many names and forms, some of which are more familiar to us than others. This fact reflects the infinite variety of expression and evolution within our Universe. If our expressions of name and form were given to another civilization in the far corners of our galaxy, they would surely bear no weight or meaning.

So, He from which all things Spiritual and Material come should be more appropriately addressed as—the One. For all things come from One, all is One, and this is the Universal concept that is true for all. So if these names or forms obstruct you in any way, by all means, disregard them. Focus on the underlying information surrounding them, which in turn will make things clearer and simpler.

For those who do not know, Lord Krishna is a two-arm expression of the One, which at any time can also express Himself in a four-arm form called Vishnu. Lord Krishna represents His ever-existing, creative feature by expanding into a form known as Lord Balarama. While the personification of His ever-new perfect Love is known as Sri Radha, His Heart.

Lord Balarama comes to create the Spiritual World by the will and power of the One. He brings forth the spiritual sky and the innumerable Vaikuntha planets—transcendental celestial abodes, full of bliss, free from duality, anxiety, lamentation, birth, and death—a place where only perfected souls may dwell.

The ruling deities of the Vaikuntha planets are all expansions of the Primordial Vishnu. They all come from His chief (first) quadruple expansions: Vasudeva, Sankarsana, Pradyumna, and Anirudha. They are all similar in form to the Original, and they give way to similar expansions that bring forth others, and so on and so forth. There are no celestial bodies of light(stars/suns) within the Spiritual Creation, for the blissful "light" of the One irradiates all.

Similarly, Sri Radha, His bliss potency, pervades and irradiates the Spiritual World. Her personality also expands into innumerable forms of Lakshmi. She is known to be the eternal consort of Vishnu, which in this case, includes all the ruling deities of the various Vaikuntha planets.

Unlike material creation, there are few certainties on this subject matter, and I don't believe there are any still bound to the material who are privy to this great mystery. The Spiritual World may have manifested expressions, or it may not, but what I perceive to be certain is that Spirit is not a fixed thing. It changes and grows, whether through what is gained in each cycle of experience or through each part of Spirit that returns to its source. These changes might be minute, but I "feel" them to be there nonetheless.

The Life and Spiritual Journey of No One

Chapter Two

Material Creation

After the creation of the Spiritual World, Lord Krishna, the supreme personality of Godhead, through and by His will and knowledge, caused Lord Balarama to act and create the material manifestation. Lord Balarama, through the figure of Sankarsana, expands into the void beyond the Spiritual World, giving way to the primordial avatar of the Lord: Maha-Vishnu (or Great Vishnu).

In much the same way, the Heart of the Lord (Krishna) follows. Sri Radha expands and goes beyond the Spiritual World as Maha-Lakshmi (or Great Lakshmi). This form then bonds with Maha-Vishnu, leading to the birth of the Material Energy (Intelligent Energy) and ultimately to the impregnation of the whole of Creation with LOVE, which will range in grade throughout. With this, the Primordial Waters (Causal Ocean/World) were cast into the void, forming Infinite Space, the primal creation of an unfathomable nature. With it comes the coil of Infinite Time (Lord Ananta), the unraveler of material creation, and the one who sets it at rest. So, whether you are a believer in a God with form or not, be sure to know that all Creation sprouts from LOVE and CONSCIOUSNESS.

After such an event, Maha-Vishnu brings into manifestation an infinite number of Universes. In Hindu scripture, it is said that they sprout from the pores of His body as He exhales, to, in time, return again with His inhaling "breath." Scientific minds would describe this as a massive singularity that, by empowering and combining various elements, sprouts into existence innumerable particle-size (bubble) Universes, including our own. These expressions maintain form for a time and dissolve back again into the singularity from which they came.

Soon after, Maha-Vishnu expands to enter, along with His creative principle, the manifold particle-sized Universes. At this point, Maha-Vishnu's expansion, now called Garbhodakaśāyī Vishnu, casts its own particular portion of the causal matrix (Causal Ocean), giving way to space and time, the canvas of life to every Universe. It is said that after such a creative act, a lotus flower began to grow from the navel of Garbhodakaśāyī Vishnu. The flower itself would become the birthplace of Lord Brahma (The Creator), while its stem would give birth to various planes of existence that unfold over the course of time (See Table 4).

The names displayed in Table 4 are quite foreign to us, but know that they do not refer to planets specifically. Instead, they depict qualities inherent to certain regions of space. For example, **Bhurloka** does not refer to planet Earth. The word conveys a mineral/earthy essence of a certain place—in other words, the physical. English translations have limitations, but I will give some more examples. **Janaloka** is said to translate to the "world of man," which is confusing. Jana conveys, in essence, the idea of a people, race, or collective. So, Janaloka refers to the fact that when a race reaches this stage of development, it usually becomes of one mind, driven by the pursuit of knowledge. **Tapoloka** is another interesting and difficult one. Tapo conveys different things that are intimately interconnected: sacred, ascetic, and austerities. It becomes a curious way of saying that in this region of space dwell the purest expressions of life. These entities do not engage in "sex." They do not eat or sleep, at least not as we understand it. This may appear dreadful to some, but they are the most beautiful expressions of life.

Table 4º - The Lotus: Arrangement within the material universe according to Hindu Scripture.

Upper Planes **(Subtle/Astral)**	Satyaloka: Lord Brahma's Abode
	Tapoloka
	Janaloka: Seven Sages
	Maharloka
	Heaven* (Heavenly planets): Home to 33 million Demigods & Demons
	Buvarloka: Rakshasa & Ghosts
Physical Plane	Bhurloka - "Earth"
Lower Planes	Atala
	Vitala
	Sutala
	Talatala
	Mahatala
	Rasatala
	Patala: Pitroloka & Hellish Planets

* - I'm sure that seeing demons in Heaven might leave most in a state of confusion, but you must understand that Heaven is just another plane of existence within our own Universe. Do not mistake the inner planes, where many souls "rest" or "heal," for the Heaven spoken of by Jesus. They are of a completely different nature, and such souls need not return to the physical.

At a certain point, Garbhodakaśāyī Vishnu expands to become Lord Brahma, Vishnu, and Shiva, creating, sustaining, and eventually dissolving His creation. This third form of Vishnu (Kṣīrodakaśāyī) is known to be the Universal form of the Lord: the transcendental, eternal overseer, sustainer, and protector of the universe, and the One who resides in everyone's heart. By now, you should have a clearer understanding of who He is, of His connection to the One, and why in the Hindu religion, He is often seen as the only "worshipable" deity. [24]

The Hindu scriptures give a clearer, more complete concept of God, and this understanding will become even clearer in time. Thus, the popular notion of multiple "Gods" is incorrect. Many are just empowered beings from a plane of existence above our own. Others embody a particular aspect of material nature, but their worship does not lead to life's ultimate goal. Some Hindu transcripts address them as demigods, which is also improper/imperfect. Still, for the sake of narrative and lessening confusion, "demigods" will be the term used throughout this book.

Don't get too tied up in this whole process. To put it simply, all these steps are just another way of saying that the Primordial Consciousness endowed each Creative Director with Love, Power, Knowledge, and Free Will to Create, each working within their own Universal "bubble."

This universal depiction might also seem strange to most, but at this point in time, I cannot completely explain it. Doing so would only give birth to even more confusion, which is not my intent. So, for now, I would just like to ask you not to take this lotus depiction too literally but to see it as a very perceptive analogy. The lotus seeds rest in the earth much like the manifold portions of Spirit (our souls). As these seeds awaken, they push through into the waters of life, reaching out ever so slowly towards the

---

[24] All these forms of Vishnu (Maha-Vishnu, Garbhodakaśāyī Vishnu, Kṣīrodakaśāyī Vishnu) are known to be the Purusha-avatars. Purusha refers to the Spirit, the infinite intelligence. The cosmic entity, Purusha, exists beyond the realms of time and space. It works and combines in steps with Prakriti, the material energy to ultimately form all material creation.

Light (the Source), and so do our souls evolve through many different bodies and different planes. Eventually, the lotus breaks through, blossoming into the Light. Similarly, our souls blossom to the Source to become all things (one with all things), ultimately leading us to transcend beyond all things. [25]

---

[25] Like so many others have done before I state that the manyfold portions of Spirit, our souls dwell in the mineral. However, this is not an exact truth. Consciousness does not have an individualized expression at this point in time. This is a factor of awareness that comes much later in the evolutionary process. In our world, such development comes firstly to more developed plant life. Trees. These forms of life come to develop a certain grade of awareness that allows them to become individualized portions of Spirit, possessors of souls, which in turn will influence their range of experience/interaction, amongst other things.

The Life and Spiritual Journey of No One

Chapter Three

Divine Mother

I have stated that Vishnu was often seen as the only "worshipable" deity in the Hindu religion. However, there might be one other that, at the very least, deserves our love, respect, and attention. She is the Goddess that leads to one's goal and resides eternally on the chest of Lord Vishnu. Thus, it can be understood that one can reach the Lord through His Heart—Lakshmi, the mother of the material universe. When I say Lakshmi, I mean Maha-Lakshmi or Her material expression.

The Divine Mother's identity is somewhat muddled, but I will try to explain. The figure of Lakshmi is a material reflection of what's already happening in the Spiritual. Her story and expression of form serve a purpose: to convey wisdom. However, circumscribing Divine Mother to a particular form, whichever it may be, becomes limiting and binding. Divine Mother is the Primordial Energy (the Maha Shakti), all-encompassing. She works side by side with Spirit, creating, maintaining, and eventually dissolving all creation. You may come to know Her more personally, but such things are not to be forced.

At one point, the One Primordial Energy expresses itself manifoldly, working multidimensionally in ways that go far beyond human comprehension. In Hinduism, there are many goddesses that sprout from the One Energy, and they are usually the female counterparts of the devas (the demigods). They are powerful manifestations of Shakti that can act toward the material or lead to the spiritual.

One can call upon these individual energies (Shaktis) through mantras, invocations, affirmations, or visualizations, and this might very well be part of your path to track, or it might not. That's for you to find out.[26]

It's curious to see that in Hindu tradition/religion, the deities have their male and female expressions. This is seen throughout Nature, including human beings, both in form and energy (Male and Female). The feminine energy is not unique to the female gender, nor is the masculine energy unique to the male form. They are in both. Male and female energies lie within all life forms (living entities) and are usually in balance, working together. However, mankind does seem to be the exception.

It's also important to understand that male and female energies are material constructs, though they are united as one in their origin. On the other hand, these constructs had their primordial origin in the Spiritual. Even if you don't believe in a personal God and see Him only as Spirit (ever-existing, ever-conscious, ever-new bliss), you will still find male energy in Its ever-conscious feature as awareness, wisdom, and reason, and female energy in Its ever-new bliss feature as pure, perfect love with its multiple grades and variations.

There are many goddesses in Hinduism, and I'm not going to dwell on them all, but to illustrate certain points, I would like to speak about two and share a little of their stories. Bear with me, and you will see that their purpose will be made clear at the end.

---

[26] The sound vibrations produced by mantras carries great power. This fact is mainly due to the language in which they are performed. Sanskrit is a language whose sound forms have a deep, undeniable connection to the primordial source of all things, as such they can bring about a greater sense of connection to the creation and to the Creator.

Lakshmi

She is considered the auspicious one (Śrí), the goddess of wealth and prosperity, and the embodiment of love, harmony, and beauty. The kind and compassionate one who bestows material and spiritual wealth. Lakshmi is accepted as the eternal consort of Vishnu, but in material creation, Her story stretches far back into time.

According to many sacred texts like the *Ramayana*, *Mahabharata*, and the Puranas, she primarily lived with the demons, blessing these worlds, their inhabitants, and rulers. However, the insatiable nature of the demons was always driving them to have more, to conquer the three Worlds. At one point, Lakshmi grew tired of this and left for the heavenly abodes of the demigods. They were the exact opposite of the demons. They were content in their position. They never strived to conquer anything, so for a long time, she bestowed her blessings on the heavenly planes.

As time passed, she realized that the demigods were very proud of their opulence and position. They were full of self-importance, arrogant, and very much afraid of losing their position. Lakshmi began to grow weary of this, and a certain event became the tipping point that determined her departure from these subtle realms.

As the story goes, a somewhat temperamental Sage named Durvasa was wandering the "Earth" when he beheld a special garland of flowers that was being held by a celestial nymph. Determining it to be divine, the Sage immediately demanded it from the nymph, who graciously and respectfully conceded. Placing the garland on himself, the Sage continued on his journey. Later on, he beheld Indra riding on his elephant Airávata. The Sage then decided to gift the garland to Indra and threw it to him. The king of the devas caught it and placed it on Airávata's head. Attracted by the smell, the elephant grabbed it and inadvertently threw it to the ground.

Such an act set the Sage on fire, who saw all this as a sign of disrespect and said:

"- Inflated with the intoxication of power, Vásava, vile of spirit, thou art an idiot not to respect the garland I presented to thee, which was the dwelling of Fortune (Śrī). Thou hast not acknowledged it as a largess; thou hast not bowed thyself before me; thou hast not placed the wreath upon thy head, with thy countenance expanding with delight. Now, fool, for that thou hast not infinitely prized the garland that I gave thee, thy sovereignty over the three worlds shall be subverted. Thou confoundest me, Śakra, with other Brahmans, and hence I have suffered disrespect from thy arrogance: but in like manner, as thou hast cast the garland I gave thee down on the ground, so shall thy dominion over the universe be whelmed in ruin. Thou hast offended one whose wrath is dreaded by all created things, king of the gods, even me, by thine excessive pride." (Wilson 149)

The king of the devas (demigods) tried to appease Durvasa with his words and prostrations, but the Sage would not yield, for he was not known for his compassionate and forgiving heart, quite the opposite. Taking her cue from Durvasa's curse, Lakshmi departs and merges into the Ocean of Milk. From that day forth, the whole of the three worlds suffered a widespread loss of luster and vigor. Trees, vegetables, plants, and herbs withered and died; men became frail, dull-minded, greedy, and frivolous, bound by desire. There were no morals or religious expressions. In truth, misery ruled the three worlds.

The demons took up this opportunity to rage war on the demigods, who fled to take refuge in Brahma's abode. Lord Brahma, after carefully assessing the situation, determined that the best course of action would be to petition aid from Lord Vishnu (Kṣīrodakaśāyī Vishnu).

After many prayers of praise and supplication given by all in attendance, Lord Vishnu appeared in great radiance. Being fully aware of the situation, the Lord said that He would replenish the strength of demigods, but they had to work side by side with the asuras (demons). Together they should uproot Mandara mountain and, depending on Him, churn the Ocean of Milk for ambrosia. To do this, the demigods had to make peace with the demons promising them an equal share of the fruits of their labor. Knowing the nature of the demons, the Lord assured the demigods that they would share in the labor alone.

The demigods were somewhat hesitant in procuring the aid of the demons, for they would sooner kill them than hear anything they had to say. Still, the Lord assured them that if they approached in humility, explained, and agreed with any terms they set, everything would be okay, and so it was.

Soon after, both parties uprooted Mandara Mountain and started carrying it toward the Ocean, but the task was overwhelming. They were almost crushed by its colossal weight were it not for the aid of Lord Vishnu, who lifted the enormous mass of land with one hand and carried it along on Garuda to the Ocean of Milk. Dropping the mountain into the Ocean, it immediately sank into its depths. At this point, the Lord expanded into **multiple forms—seen and unseen—**aiding both demigods and demons so that they could properly labor in the process. Both parties worked diligently. Soon after, wondrous things started springing out from the Ocean of Milk: the cow Surabhi, the goddess Váruní (the deity of wine), the celestial Párijáta tree, the cool-rayed Moon. Surprisingly, even poison was brought forth, followed by the nectar of immortality (Amrita) and, finally, Lakshmi. She rose in great radiance and beauty from the depth of the Ocean; devas (demigods) and asuras were entranced by the goddess, and all desired to have her for themselves. However, Lakshmi turned to Lord Vishnu, casting herself into His chest as a symbol of their union.

The story goes on, but what's been said is enough to illustrate the points I want to make. Lakshmi's "life" and journey show her all-pervading nature in creation. Her union with Vishnu at the end shows her rightful place, a testament to harmony and cooperation between Spirit and Nature. From that point onward, a balance was established between the forces of light and darkness, neither gaining prevalence over the other. That journey to union is also an important message to the self-aware: realize that the path to the One is the Heart—Love. [27]

---

[27] For those who follow the path of Love and Light, unlocking the heart (chakra) is key in that process, and I've certainly felt and seen it. I was "stuck" doing work at the heart for quite some time. I could literally see it, for every time I practiced, a round red patch would appear dead center on my chest. This mark eventually faded away, and as it did, an increasing surge of energy was felt, flowing up to my higher centers.

Sita and Dharma

The story of Sita is, if nothing else, a lesson on Dharma. In the Ramayana, she and Rama, an avatar of Lord Vishnu, play out a complex drama for the benefit of mankind. This story is rich in content, full of lessons that sometimes can be misunderstood or, at the very least, not fully comprehended—which is often the case in most scripture.

So, what is Dharma? It's impossible to give a linear definition of this concept, so I won't even try. Notwithstanding, I will strive to weave together a set of ideas and appropriate examples to give some level of understanding of it. Even so, I feel that anything I do will fall short of accurately depicting such a complex, dynamic, living concept.

While growing up, I was bound by honor. It was something that stuck with me for as long as I can remember, but when I was asked to explain it, I couldn't. It wasn't justice, virtue, morality, or duty, although all these concepts lived within it. Dharma is an even more encompassing concept; one might say it to be the way of righteousness, but still, this explains little. What is, in fact, right, and what is wrong? This is no simple question, as we live in a world of multiple shades and grades. This is exactly where dharma comes into play. Most of the time, there is no 100% right nor 100% wrong, and the best we can hope for is to lean toward the right side as much as we possibly can.

Dharma is part of a path more in tune with the True Nature of Creation, and acting according to it results from being in a certain state of awareness (consciousness). Self-realized souls inadvertently act according to dharma and often confound conditioned souls who consider their actions to be contradictory. Not being a self-realized soul should not keep you from acting according to dharma, and if you strive to think and act with a sense of inclusiveness, you might just be closer to where you need to be. Realize that you are no more important or deserving than anyone else. Include different life forms in your way of thinking, and include the World. Let's look at the Ramayana to give some examples and illustrate some points.

The Life and Spiritual Journey of No One

In the Ramayana, both Ram (Rama) and Sita are of noble, virtuous character. He is one of four sons, the pride and joy of His father Dasharatha, king of Kosala, and she is one of two sisters, daughter to Mother Earth and King Janaka, a God-realized soul. Through the way of challenge, Rama later united in matrimony with Sita; the challenge was put forth by King Janaka to find a worthy suitor for Sita. It implied lifting and stringing Shiva's bow, a mighty weapon few could bear to look upon, and fewer still could even budge from its position. Ram, being an avatar of the Lord, felt no difficulty. In fact, the mighty bow broke in His hands, sending a powerful shock wave throughout the land.

The divine couple then began living happy lives in Ayodhya (the kingdom's capital). If ever there was a perfect household, this was it. There was no enmity or envy. Everyone was a reflection of virtue and morality, but soon this would all change, and clouds of misfortune would fall upon the kingdom. King Dasharatha decided that it was time to proclaim Ram crown prince of the kingdom. As such, he ordered that preparations be made to have an official ceremony as soon as possible. Hearing this, an old maidservant of Queen Kaikeyi panicked. Out of fear of losing her position, she started turning the queen's mind, who up until then had nothing but love for Ram (her stepson).

The maid said: "This dreadful situation could yet be avoided if you asked for the boons (wishes of sorts) you were given long ago. Just make sure to secure his vow to fulfill your desires before you ask. After you've done so, ask the King to proclaim your son Bharata crown prince and to exile Ram to the forest for fourteen years, giving enough time for the people to love Bharata as a ruler." By this time, the queen's mind was so distorted that she was all too willing to do so. In the end, Ram went into exile, followed by Lakshmana (his brother) and Sita, leaving behind a kingdom filled with despair.

This is a recurrent theme in Hindu scripture. Being true to your word is dharma, but not always. Many might be thinking: *"What are you saying? Should I not be truthful?"*

First of all, one should always refrain from vowing/promising rashly. In fact, one should quit these practices altogether, especially when they give their recipient such a wide range of choices. This, most often than not, puts the giver and others in harm's way.

When you use words like "I Swear ...", "I Vow..." and "I Promise..." it is to emphasize the truth in your words, but truthful men do not need to resort to such things, nor do others demand it of them, for it is in their nature to do so. Understand that these vows often sprout out of a sense of pride and confidence in the conditioned self; secondly, truth should never be spoken neglectfully. It may hurt others or yourself. Sometimes it's better to be silent. While doing so, the right thing to say might just come to you, but there may be times when these are not an option, and you may be forced to speak truthfully or untruthfully. If and when you choose to do the latter, just make sure that you're doing it for the right reason(s) and not for your own self-interest.

Continuing with our story: Ram was now living a peaceful, happy life in the forest. He found solace in Sita and Lakshmana, and they found comfort in Him, but this, as it turns out, was to be short-lived. A demon king named Ravana, who wreaked havoc on the three worlds, heard from his sister of the incomparable beauty of Sita. Being one filled with desire, he immediately plotted to make her his own. Eventually, he kidnapped Sita, inadvertently setting the two brothers on a quest to get her back. After a long journey filled with adventure, tribulation, and death, Ram finally defeated Ravana and saved Sita. However, upon setting his sights on her, Ram said that it was not for love or affection that He fought and struggled but for the sake of his family's honor. He said:

> *"My love is fled, for on thy fame*
> *Lies the dark blot of sin and shame;*
> *And thou art hateful as the light*
> *That flashes on the injured sight.*
> *The world is all before thee: flee:*
> *Go where thou wilt, but not with me." (Griffith* 1749-1750*)*

Of course, Sita was undeserving of such words. However, you have to understand that Ram (an avatar of Lord Vishnu) was playing His part in this drama to illustrate a way of thinking, a way of doing, that is still very much alive. In a broader sense, He showed how sometimes we do the right thing for the wrong reasons, which is key in dharma. The thought behind the act is more important than the act itself.

Sita was gone for a year, and Ravana was known for his insatiable sexual desires that showed no restraint. Whenever he desired a woman, he would take her willingly or unwillingly. This way of acting led Ravana to be cursed by a demigod, so he was to never force himself on another under penalty of death, but this fact was known to very few. Still, this is beside the point. Saving Sita was right in itself. Even if she had fallen victim to such an act, what would be her fault? She didn't ask or want any of it. Wouldn't she require more love, compassion, and understanding if that were the case? Sita suffered many misfortunes, but this was not one of them. She lived in a way that no fault could be found in her, even by those of the most fixed minds.

Ram's words pierced Sita like sharp shafts. She was stunned in disbelief, pained by His words. She tearfully asked if He had forgotten her character, her conduct in life. She continuously addressed Ram, asking what fault could be found in her, but Ram remained unflinching. Sita then asked that a large pyre be built so she may enter. Hearing this, Lakshmana wistfully gazed at Ram, but still, He remained unfazed. In fact, no chieftain dared question His stern posture. With the fire now blazing into the sky, Sita prayed with folded hands. She said:

> *"As this fond heart by virtue swayed*
> *From Raghu's son has never strayed,*
> *So, universal witness, Fire*
> *Protect my body on the pyre,*
> *As Raghu's son has idly laid*
> *This charge on Sítá, hear and aid."* (Griffith 1752)

Loud cries rang out from the crowd as Sita entered the fire. The piercing cries dragged out Ram's true feelings, and tears outwardly expressed the sadness He was already feeling inside. At this point in time, a divine band of celestials (demigods) descended from the heavens, upholders of truth set on defending Sita's honor. Bearing witness to her purity, the lord of Fire emerged with Sita from the pyre, unscathed and radiant. In the end, Sita reunited with Ram. Finally, He was able to receive her with open arms and no restrictions.

A while after returning to the city of Ayodhya, unflattering rumors began to spread amongst the people. This gossip was filled with allegations of Sita being touched by Ravana, which according to religious tradition, left her unfit to be the king's wife. This gossip eventually reached Ram's ears, leaving Him plagued by an overwhelming amount of anxiety, which ultimately led Him to exile His pregnant wife to the forest.

Ram was trying to act according to dharma by sacrificing His wife and children. He was striving to uphold religious principles, trying to give the right example for the sake of the people, but this act resulted from faulty reasoning. Is it dharma to act in accordance with the belief of others? People are prone to believe whatever they want, no matter what you say or what you do, but should you be conditioned by it? No. If it were so, Ram wouldn't have left for the forest in the first place. Everyone thought it wrong and urged Him to dethrone the king, to fight back and take what was rightfully His, but He didn't. Even after His father's death, when Bharata went to the forest to give Him the kingdom, He still would not budge. The life of Christ is also a living testament to this truth. Dharma is not bound by popular belief, nor is it bound by fixed constructs like law, tradition, or even religion.

So, you might ask, is it not right to sacrifice one for the sake of the many? It might, but let me ask you this: Is it a sacrifice for you to make? People are often keen on sacrificing others under the guise of righteousness when in fact, such words and actions spring from of a selfish sense of self-preservation.[28]

On the other hand, wouldn't unilaterally sacrificing others defile the righteous act one is trying to uphold? What would be the meaning behind Jesus Christ's sacrifice if it were not a willing one? These are just some examples, but things are not so simple. Following dharma may imply acting differently according to the makeup of a situation and the people involved. That is why being in the right state of consciousness is so important. Those who do not dwell in high states of consciousness, with a greater sense of inclusiveness (unity), are prone to make mistakes (see Appendix II), and that's OK. It's all part of the process.

Fortunately, Sita found shelter in the hermitage of a sage named Valmiki, who kindly offered to take care of her and her unborn children. She lived a simple, peaceful life in the forest, caring and instructing her children (Kusa & Lava) with the affectionate help of the sage. Years later, by fate's design, Ram caught sight of His children. This fleeting encounter roused a deep longing in His heart. Too long had He been away from His beloved Sita. Ram became overwhelmed by thoughts of reuniting with Sita and of living together for the rest of their lives. Fixed in mind, the King sent Lakshmana to summon the former queen back to their court. Sita arranged herself beautifully, putting on garments and ornaments, things she hadn't worn since the day of her exile. Upon meeting Ram, Sita decided to reaffirm her innocence one last time. She said with a shaking heart:

"If, in thought, I have never dwelt on any but Rama,
may the Goddess Madhavi (Mother Earth) receive me!"

(Shastri, *Book 7- 617*)

---

[28] Life is indeed precious, and more so in man, but it always surprises me to see so many clinging to life in this world, even to the point of seeking immortality. We have been dying since the day of our birth. Death just comes sooner to some and later to others. It's inevitable, so the only true question is how much "baggage" we take when we go.

A large earthquake started rumbling across the land, the ground opened up, and out came Mother Earth, sitting on a throne surrounded by Nagas. She motioned affectionately to Sita, inviting her to come. With a gentle embrace, Mother Earth took her back. Ram could do nothing more than watch in disbelief as the ground softly closed up behind them, never to open again.

In India, some consider Sita to be the ideal wife, submissive, loyal, and chaste. However, I do not consider submissiveness a quality, nor blind loyalty for that matter, and Sita is not guilty of being either. The first thing we must remember is who her parents and husband were, in fact, all her close relationships in life. There are few in this world with such straight moral compasses, be they parents, brothers, sisters, husbands, wives, etc. Sita always acted accordingly. If she were guilty of being submissive, she wouldn't have denied Ravana, which she did, even under threat of torture and death. Nor would she have denied Ram in the end. Instead of returning to the one she loved, she chose to depart from the Earth in a revealing act, giving testimony to her righteous conduct in life. Yes, Sita was the perfect wife, kind, compassionate, brave, supportive, and forbearing. Still, just like Mother Nature, if one continues to neglect and disrespect her, she will inadvertently depart, turn from you, from us in one way or another.

Heroes

The concept of the hero is indeed a strange and interesting one. The Ramayana is, in a more objective sense, the tale and portrait of a hero, but what is, in fact, a hero? Heroes are seen as figures of power and strength, admired for their courage and outstanding achievements. The word itself seems to label them as champions of right. Still, in this world, one man's hero is often another man's villain, so how can this be true**?** The hero concept remains relevant and significant in this plane of existence. As such, I will endeavor to bring it to new light.

So what is, in fact, a hero? What makes "you" a hero? I would say that heroes are all those that always strive to do what's "right" despite whatever difficulties they face. Their actions always tend to kindle the spirit of others in a very positive way, but let's put this in parts. Strength and power do not make you a hero. In fact, strong and powerful people rarely do what's "right," even when it's easy. Bravery is not indispensable, but some courage is sometimes required to do the right thing. In regard to achievements, the first thing to consider is the "true" nature of what we speak. Secondly, I would like to say that success is not a real measure of a hero. If one tries his utmost and fails, should he be considered any less? There are many definitions of the word hero, but they all seem to lack what truly makes a real hero—the quality that should be prevalent in all heroes: **love**.

Maya

Maya is a Hindu concept that portrays material Mother Nature as an "illusion," as something not real, ultimately nothing. I cannot say that this concept is not ultimately true, but conveying things in this manner may lead one to see no real purpose or meaning to this world, to life. This concept can leave most in a state of confusion. Some will come to renounce the world, while others will find themselves in a state of apathy. So what real benefit is derived from teaching this concept? We might say that our universe is nothing more than a projection of light that spreads out multi-dimensionally, much like different grades of holographic projections. However, knowing this does not exclude one from playing the "game of life."

We all have to experience, learn, and evolve through many expressions of life**. You** might choose to ignore this truth, but there's no running from it. At times, those on the spiritual path disregard material nature for not being the ultimate reality or for some other reason constructed in their minds, but this will unavoidably obstruct them from where they need to be. One cannot move forward without accepting and embracing all aspects of the One, for all is One.

You should also realize that all spiritual practices are material, not "Spiritual." Meditation, Kriya, other forms of pranayama, mantras, fasting, our thoughts, and even our dreams are all material in nature. They are called spiritual because they bring us ever closer to Spirit — and not for any other reason.

Chapter Four

Lord Krishna – The Mellows

From time to time, the Lord comes to this plane of existence in different ways and forms, usually to experience and enact certain roles. Most of the time, He does so to guide, give, and protect. Some will say that God is fully content in Himself and has no need to enjoy/experience anything else. Although this is true, it's not the absolute truth, for if it were so, what need would there be to create anything at all**?** There are also those who will say that the coming of the Lord onto "Earth" is impossible. To those who state such a thing, I would like to say that connecting impossibility to the One is contradictory, to say the least. Still, in a deeper sense, I would like to ask those who think this way to introspect and ascertain the veracity of this statement for themselves.

My intent here is not to dwell in great depth on the life of Krishna. That would be something far too difficult and complex to approach in any one book. What follows is just a view from a fragment in scripture, but I deem it important, especially for those acquainted with this concept (the mellows). As such, I reiterate the importance of reading such works as part of your journey.

Some devotees strive to connect with the One by nurturing a more personalized connection. In India, these are called mellows of devotional service. There are many mellows, but the principal ones are servitude, friendship, parental affection, and conjugal love. Seeing God as a father and/or mother is also an important mellow, but it falls into the category of servitude as we are always the "eternal servants" of our parents. Note that this is just a figure of speech used to illustrate an idea; it does not make you a slave to anyone.

Krishna's life is seen as a direct experience of these mellows, especially the early years of a purer, simpler time in His life. However, despite the best efforts of a few, these mellows continue to puzzle but hopefully not for long.

The Mellows:

Servitude

In the mellow of servitude, the devotee strives to serve the Lord in whichever way he can, but this mellow is often followed by fear that arises within his heart, which creates distance between the Lord and himself. I could never understand the popular expression: "I'm a God-fearing man." How about becoming a God-loving man instead**?** What kind of relationship is founded on fear? Look at your own relationships, and the answer will become clear. This sense of service is present in all other mellows, for aren't we all but servants of the One**?**

Friendship

In this mellow, the devotee strives to create a deeper connection with the Lord. He desires to casually speak with Him, to sport, embrace, defend, and serve Him. He longs to share in His exploits, adventures, and wanderings. In Vrindavan, Subal embodied the purest form of this mellow (as children), but Arjuna's friendship with the Lord always moved me in a particular way. Balarama participates in Krishna's pastimes as brother and friend, but He does not take part in the mellows. He remains fully aware of His position and Lord Krishna's identity. This is not so for all the others. Especially in Vrindavan, they live and experience the opulence of the Lord but are too engrossed in their mellows to "notice."

Parental Affection

In this mellow, the devotees desire to nurture/sustain, protect, teach, and even chastise the Lord. This is a rather complicated mellow to nurture, more so for men than women. Although mellows may evolve from one into another, the seeds of such a particular love should already be in the devotee. Similarly, not all those with children are fit to be parents, whether fathers or mothers. Deity worship might be a good way to aid in this process, but this will come much more naturally to Indians than Westerners. In this mellow, Krishna plays the part of a conditioned soul allowing Mother Yashoda to live it to her heart's content. He is restless and reckless, so she worries and protects Him. He steals, acts mischievously, and irrationally. Subsequently, she teaches and chastises Him, but she also rejoices in holding, feeding, and bathing Krishna. The mere memory of His expressions, sounds, and activities stirs her heart.

Conjugal Love

This is a mellow of friendship in intimacy where the devotee seeks to enjoy a loving relationship with the Lord. There were many female devotees (gopis) with whom Lord Krishna enjoyed His pastimes, but Radha stood above the rest. As such, I will mostly focus on Her. We should first understand that by His supreme potency, the Lord caused Sri Radha to descend on "Earth" without consciousness of who She really was. As a result, She felt like She had found Her long-lost soul mate in Krishna (Her eternal love). By such action, the Lord was able to enjoy His heart without the conditioning caused by the consciousness of position. Radha and Krishna share a familiarity that deeply transcends that incarnation. As such, many see this mellow as a purer expression of Primordial Love.

This mellow is an "endless" courting process, with its varied dynamics and experiences: dancing, walking, sitting, holding hands, embracing, flirting, sleeping, and kissing. However, from time to time, Radha would display fake anger and jealousy. She'd resist His embrace, pretend to ignore Him, but in Her heart, all She wanted to do was reconcile. Among their elders, they would often exchange secret glances with each other, which in turn brought pleasure and anxiety within their hearts.

All other gopis wanted nothing more than to share in these pastimes and feelings. As such, by the symbolic act of stealing all their clothes while they were bathing, the Lord accepted their affection. At times the gopis are referred to as being "lusty" toward Krishna. This is an expression used to convey a powerful desire to satisfy the Lord; it has no sexual connotation whatsoever. The pleasure of the devotees derives only from the act of pleasing the Lord in different ways, according to the nature of each mellow. In sum, it is the act of giving unconditionally to another. Activities like sleeping together or kissing often trigger judgment in the readers' minds, which in turn obstructs them. In Vrindavan, the act of sleeping together refers to the actual act of sleeping, not sex.[29]

In Dwarka, Lord Krishna did marry and have children. His wives' desire arose not from material taint but from a natural "worldly" desire to satisfy the One they love and to bear His children. Kissing is a whole different matter. Although intimate, it's not sexual. It's personal, special, and very much a part of the courting process.

When Krishna departed from Vrindavan, it was like life was taken from them. The higher the mellow, the deeper the pangs of separation within the devotee, but Radha felt this more than most. This was, of course, Divine Love, from which all other forms and expressions of love derive. Those rare couples who share a link of a golden thread can see and feel a measure of it, for they bear with difficulty even little moments of separation but have an even harder time when they see themselves parted by death.

---

[29] Some of the stories about Krishna in Vrindavan stir the minds of those who read them. It may come to still the minds of many to know that Krishna at the time was no more than 9 or 10 years old, but know that in time you will come to go beyond this way of thinking. We all have inherited biases regarding age, gender, color, etc. These biases can be more or less distorted, some more deeply rooted than others, but they are in all of us, making us see, think, and act in a certain way. You will realize that the Consciousness dwelling in Krishna is not bound by concepts of age or anything else. This may help in understanding His words and actions, which often confound many.

The Essence Behind the Mellows

The perspective given in and by these mellows has been expounded in a similar fashion in other literary works, and I must say that it's not without its value, but I think it fails to see the greater picture. We analyze and focus so much that we fail to see things as a whole. This form of exposition expresses, in some ways, certain forms of human interaction but fails to address, in full, its varieties and complexities. On the other hand, it dismisses almost completely the most important point of view—Krishna's. One should always strive to see the divine presence in others, expressing love and understanding in whatever measure we can. At times those expressions can be more "close," open, and pure, as seen between those who live in a brighter light, whether they be lovers or friends. In others, love and understanding have to be given silently, at times from afar, as we cannot condone certain ways of thinking and acting.

One could go on and on about different grades of expression in different levels of human interaction, but whatever they may be, what one feels at heart should never change. This reminds me of a curious moment with my wife.

One day she asked with interest, "**Do you love our neighbor's child as much as our own?**"

I replied, "**Yes, I love them the same.**"

With an expression of annoyance she said, "**No, you don't. You shouldn't say such things.**"

I understand her confusion. In her mind, our child should be number one, and my statement may have seemed derogatory towards him, but I assure you it was not. The expression of love is a factor of opportunity and consciousness, and I use the term consciousness in the sense that we are all limited by how each individual can give and receive love. Let me explain by taking my cue from the dialogue above.

My predisposition to love is the same, so I love my neighbor's child as much as my own. What I lack is just the opportunity to show it. What I mean is that I'm unable to express certain forms of love due to my position. I do not play the father's role, nor does that child see me as such. That's the only real difference. There is no real issue here. In this world, we are given different opportunities to experience and express love in different forms/ways. Such is the gift of the One. Please note that this should not be confused with a way of weighing and/or measuring love. In essence, we can only grade a form of human interaction according to the purity of its expression.

Still, more often than not, we fail to cherish this gift, and this is due to the consciousness dwelling in each. We are usually bent on receiving, waiting, and wanting to experience love in whatever way or form, but this is not the proper frame of mind. To experience love, someone has to express it. If no one expresses it, none will experience it. On the other hand, we are also limited by the individual's ability to perceive and receive. From what's been given, you can extrapolate to all other forms of interaction, human or otherwise. For me, we are all number one. We are all One. I think I've always felt and thought in this way; I just didn't realize it.

Chapter Five

The Modes of Material Nature (The Gunas)

For those that are very much "involved" in this world, oneness is truly a difficult concept to see and/or understand, for this world is filled with confusion and polar opposites that, most of the time, leave us at a loss. Some find no meaning to it, and others care not to find any. The Lord's creation is said to be the play of the One (God). This, of course, leaves most people more confused than before and sometimes dwelling in a state of anger. "Play, you say? Does He find entertainment in our misery?" Of course, this is not the case; deep within yourself, you know it too. The material universe is, in essence, God knowing itself through different grades of consciousness, expression, and experience. Without the existence of polarity and confusion, there would be no point to the material creation, for every individual spark would perceive nothing but Unity. As such, there would be no real experience to be had. There would be only love and understanding throughout.

In the Hindu scriptures, there is a concept named the modes of material nature, or gunas. They are, in essence, three and refer specifically to this plane of existence but not just to this plane. These modes of material nature are a simple way of portraying different stages of choice or states of development that lead to that choice (evolution). [30]

---

[30] The Sanskrit word Guna can be translated as meaning "quality, attribute, property."

The translated version of the three modes of nature is as follows: the mode of goodness (sattva), the mode of passion (rajas), and the mode of ignorance (tamas). In these translations, I can only agree with the one given to rajas. I consider the translation for sattva to be inappropriate and the one given to tamas to be both "unfortunate" and misleading. As such, I will use terminology more appropriate to the proper meaning of the words: sattva as light and tamas as darkness.

Those souls who we might call younger are usually born in the mode of passion. They long to experience, to have, and to do. They are filled with desire and appear to show a sort of contentment in the way of things. As a soul grows older in experience, it starts to develop a weariness for this world, seeing no order or sense to it. At this point, the individual embarks on one of two paths: that of light or darkness. Often, this choice is made long before one has conscious awareness of it.

Those who choose light might come to find difficulty, especially in the early stages of their choice. Those who are bent toward the dark tend to harm themselves as much as others. However, as time goes by, they will embark on a more conscious and controlled fashion in following the way of the negative, using all others for the benefit and satisfaction of the self. Those who strive for a brighter light do so feebly and imperfectly in the beginning. As such, they are bound to stumble and make "mistakes," but they will eventually find their place with the help of many. There are no definites, only when the choice is set in "stone." Before that, a different path might be taken at any moment, and such change might be of an extreme nature.

There are general characterizations of the three modes of nature, but they have very little value. They fail to see that every mode has almost an infinite number of grades. They fail to speak of their interactions and influence on the life experience of the self-aware. Nor do they speak of how they change and evolve over time. Let us take some examples to illustrate at least some of what I speak: For instance, those in the mode of light are said to be peaceful, pure, and virtuous, but these are traits of those pretty much established in the light. For the most part, those who find themselves in the very beginning long only to be and express these things. As you can guess, from one end to the other, there are almost infinite degrees where one might find himself in.

Things are similar in the mode of darkness, but there are differences. Often enough, one finds himself in a dark place not by real choice but due to circumstance. Many feel like there's no other way to live. Still, for most, we can just say that: *"...they know not what they do."* (Luke 23:34). As such, I would caution all against labeling anyone as being dark or evil. We should only see thoughts, words, and actions as positive or negative in nature. Notwithstanding, predominance in one will indeed, over time, lead a soul to travel on a certain path.

In Hindu scripture, those in the mode of darkness are often depicted as imbalanced, lazy, anxious, and depressed, but this is only true for those who find themselves in the primal stages of influence. Not so for those who actively follow the negative path. Those who persist in the negative way start to see and act differently. They treasure and nurture themselves with great care. They are in control, usually very focused and sharp, seeing everything else as tools to serve the self.

Most of us dwell in the middle, in the mode of passion. Sometimes leaning towards the light and sometimes bending to the dark, but never in any definite path. We must, however, acknowledge that for the human race, it is much easier to sink into some form of darkness than to see us swimming in any grade of light. These souls will continue to linger in the middle until such time as they decide to do differently, whenever that may be.

Conditioned Souls

As we are brought deeper into the light, a longing of a different nature starts to grow within us. We start playing a different game in life, or if you prefer, we start playing the game of life differently. Still, the mixed nature of this world does not make this an easy venture.

"Why do people act the way they do?" we wonder.

We often struggle to deal with others. We fail to understand them, making it hard to maintain the underlying idea of oneness in our hearts and minds. The conditioned soul cannot help but act, speak, or think in a certain way, and the key word here is "conditioned." The mode(s) of nature in a particular soul condition it to feel, think, speak, and act in a determined way in a specific situation or circumstance. This fact is directly related to the centers of consciousness in man, the chakras. They are centers from which experience is perceived and processed. Each entity processes experience in accordance with the development of its own centers.

As a general rule, only the primary three centers are open in man. However, some may come to unlock higher centers, allowing experience to be perceived and processed in a different light. So, you should understand that you are in that very same process and that you've been in that very same place. This simple fact should foster understanding, not judgment. This refers not just to the early stages of development but to every stage of our development in this plane of existence. In past lifetimes, we have found ourselves in those very same circumstances, and we've made those very same "mistakes," we just lost awareness of it.

There will be those who will have a hard time accepting what's been said. They will profess themselves to be firm believers in free will, rejecting such concepts as fate or destiny, but my friend, aren't these two sides of the same coin?

I would like to state that this is not the be-all and end-all. We are in a plane of existence that is itself full of complexities, and as we move toward the end of this book, things will be made clear. You'll see a fundamental choice to be made by each and every one of you (of us). Those who are reading this book have already made it. You're just striving to bring it more into the light of wisdom (understanding).

I would also like to take this opportunity to advise caution. Love and compassion should always be guided by wisdom. Avoid those whose minds are not in tune with your own and with your goals. If such souls unavoidably cross your path, it is due to providence, and there is something to give or take from it. When a soul of light is born into this world, it feels misplaced, in a completely foreign world to its nature, but these souls are not forgotten. No one soul is forgotten, and no one goes without help.

The Life and Spiritual Journey of No One

Chapter Six

The Yuga's - The Cycles of Time

There are many cycles of time within creation. However, as given in scripture, the yugas pertain to the plane of existence of the Self-aware (men). This is a somewhat complex subject and full of confusion. If this was done on purpose or not, I cannot say. Trying to use what is given in scripture to explain certain concepts and ideas is bound to complicate things, but I will try to use what I can, mainly for the benefit of those who already know these concepts.

What in scripture is considered a cycle (Yuga cycle) actually is not. A cycle is something that comes full circle, something that repeats itself after a predetermined period of time. So, for the sake of understanding, let's say that the Yugas come in cycles of 24,000 years (a Full Cycle), divided into ascending and descending arcs of 12,000 years each (See Table 5 & Diagram 4). Some consider these to be Earth years, and others do not, giving way to further confusion. On the other hand, there seems to be a discrepancy between civilizations regarding the lengths of these cycles. The Hindus say 24,000, the Mayans 26,000, and the Egyptians 25,000. I have found that the problem lies in attempting to explain, linearly, something that's not linear at all: the concepts of time and space.

The higher consciousness that bestowed this knowledge to these different civilizations hailed from different corners of Creation, which in turn makes the process of factoring in a proper timeline that much more difficult.

Let me explain by using our own solar system as an example. What constitutes a day, a year? And for what planet? This can differ quite a bit. One year for Neptune is about 165 Earth years. Now, if you factor in higher planes of existence and different regions of our Universe, you can see how much more complicated this can be. So, from here on out, I will use the timeline given to the Egyptians, not just because I think it is closer to fact but because it's familiar to me. Also, to make it clear, all these timelines were given in Earth years. It would make no sense to do it any other way.

Table 5° - Length of each age (yuga). The sum of these is considered a Yuga cycle, an ark in Hindu scriptures.

Age (for Westerners)	Yuga (for Hindus)	Duration (Years)
4 - Golden Age (Highest)	4 - Satya Yuga (Highest)	4 800
3 - Silver Age	3 - Treta Yuga	3 600
2 - Bronze Age	2 - Dwapara Yuga	2 400
1 - Iron Age (Lowest)	1 - Kali Yuga (Lowest)	1 200
	Σ = Yuga cycle	Σ = 12 000

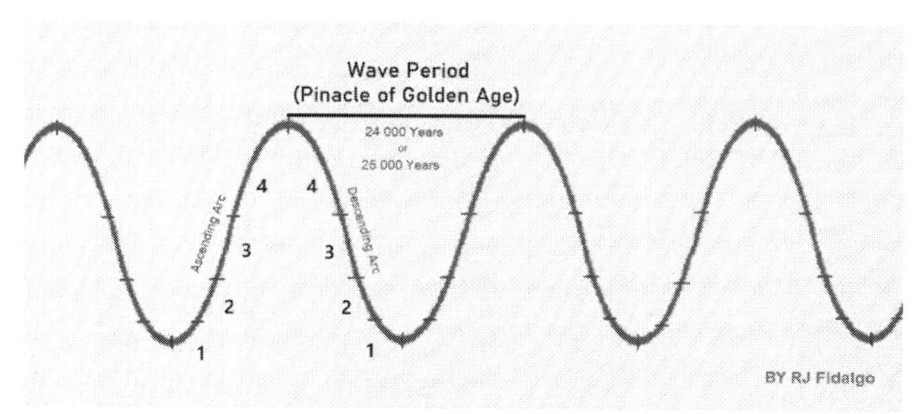

Diagram 4° - Full Cycle.

Note - In Scripture, the four ages or yugas comprise a Yuga cycle, which is not to be mistaken with the **Full cycle** of 24 000 years.

Untangling Concepts

Time is not a linear thing. It has multidimensional characteristics. The same is true about space, for as we have seen, there are multiple planes of existence. Imagine, if you can, a Universal Multidimensional Clock with multiple gears, each with its own cycles (length of revolution). As consciousness evolves on a certain planet, a new gear comes into being, clutching its spoke into a pre-existing one. In such a way, step-by-step, consciousness evolves toward the One. So, to make this clear: these 25,000-year cycles pertain to this plane of existence, to Earth, and more importantly, to the cycle of development in men.

In scripture, there are curious depictions of timelines within these cycles (the different yugas). However, such depictions fail to consider the free will of those who "live." That is to say, the conscious choices made by the self-aware, which in turn make any generalization useless. Let us take Satya Yuga as an example. In the Golden Age, it is said that all humans are kind and friendly, that there is no crime, and religion is one. Everyone is spiritually advanced, long-living, well-built, honest, youthful, vigorous, learned, and virtuous. This is said with absolute certainty, as if there were none with the free choice to do otherwise, which is not true. The ways of the light always respect the free will of others, be it to ignore or to turn the other way.

What's important to note is that at one point, we are closer to the source, and as the wheel of time turns, we grow further away to return again to that very same place. There is undoubtedly a "peak" in this wheel, but this is more a window of opportunity than a point. It stretches over a period of time, which is very hard to determine with precision. At this point, there are certainly more favorable conditions/opportunities for the self-aware entity (man) to evolve, but by his choice, man is free to completely disregard them.

Every gear that comes into existence begins its revolution from the "top," from the point closest to the source. Mind you, that this does not mean that the final goal is there. Think of it this way, there are many gears, and one builds up on the other like a staircase, each one bringing us closer to the goal (The One). It's also important to note that this is also a spatial revolution, for time and space are intricately interconnected. To complicate things, other gears/cycles interconnect and influence our own. Eventually, all connect to a Master Gear, which holds time for the whole of the Universe.

We are now in a crucial moment, for I believe we are again at that point nearest to the source. Many loving souls have worked and are working still to make us ready. May we acknowledge the opportunity and try to do better. There will be those with a certain level of scriptural (Hindu) background who won't fully accept what is stated above. They will say that according to such and such calculations/determination, this cannot be true, but dear friend, I do not force you to believe or accept anything. However, I believe that most of you are working under an erroneous notion.

The life of Krishna, Rama, and other scriptural texts are not of this Cycle of Creation. At that time, the law of Free Will was seen "somewhat differently," and this statement alone will suffice for the grasp of a few. To others, this may come later, along with its full range of underlying meanings. Mind you, that this fact does not diminish the value of Hindu scripture, on the contrary. What a gift. What a gift, indeed. On the other hand, I would like to state that these scriptures (miracles) were given to Earth and to these people with due cause. There are no mistakes. One should not even undermine the language in which they were given. Such sounds were never meant to be used casually or dismissively.

It is very difficult to determine the end of this shift in space/time-time/space because this is in part subordinate to the overall stage of development of our collective consciousness as a planet. However, the divine granted me a glimpse of the current state of things. It came to me in a dream, which I understood almost immediately.

I was in a room, and on the floor of this room was a large blanket (**white and soft**). On it were babies arranged in two rows of five. They were all nicely snuggled in white sheets.

Picture 7º - Arrangement of newborns.

My wife was there, and one other person, whom I cannot identify. I was inspecting the babies: two had half-opened eyes and good features, which I deemed a good sign. The baby on their right was radiant and full of joy. His eyes were wide open, and he grabbed my fingers, pulling himself up. At this point, the other figure in the room said: "**He's already been chosen.**"

After this, I continued to let my gaze pass over the others. They were all sleeping soundly, indistinct from one another, but the three on the far-left showed signs and features which I considered very inauspicious.

The meaning is as follows:

At this point in time (**2020**), **10%** of those who are born into this world are those already chosen to go to whatever upper plane they belong to. These are souls that, by their own will, choose to come to Earth for the benefit of others—to serve as beacons of light, love, and harmony. About **20%** are those who might be brought well into the light, for they are well-established in that path. The large majority, **40%,** are those in the mode of passion, driven to live life to the fullest. The remaining **30%** are those of the negative (dark)—those of self-interest, born to disrupt, to bring discord, and disharmony. [31]

After I finished my observations, my wife said, "**Just choose already. They are all the same.**"

I felt rather annoyed by this statement, for I knew this was not true. We are all the same in the eyes of the One, for we are all His children, but each soul has its own grade of development.

I then left, thinking to myself: *"All the same! ALL THE SAME! Pff... Nonsense."* As I did so, a group of people very cordially and joyously said goodbye and thank you. I replied in kind, which left me in a very good mood.

---

[31] This truth is also a testimony to balance between light and darkness, as equal opportunity is given to both (30%).

Chapter Seven

The Way Back: (Roads of Consciousness)

The usual depiction of our universe and the encasement of our souls in three bodies always left me uneasy. Something was off. It did not feel like I was taking part in an evolutionary process. What I did feel, in fact, was that I was put in a multidimensional prison with little hope of escape. Now, was this a product of my perception or a result of how this knowledge was conveyed? Is there a difference? Is this one of those very same subtle forms of teaching through the negative, or is it due to a very fundamental law? Something to reflect upon.

Realizing what I've stated above, I decided to convey truth without the weight of previous understandings, to do it simply and clearly, or at least as much as possible while dwelling on such complex subjects. As such, I will start within our universe and work my way down and up from there.

The Creator initially casts His consciousness into the four directions. He then, through portions of Himself, brings into being nebulae, stars, planetary systems, and galaxies that grow and make up our universe. This is, of course, a broad depiction of something that takes a very long time to come about. Slowly but surely, multiple parts of that pure creative consciousness (stars) come to bring about this larger expression of "life" (galaxy).

Think of stars as independent subcontractors, each one responsible for the development/experience of their own multidimensional planetary system. These subcontractors are endowed with Free Will to direct their little portion of creation, but they are nevertheless connected with the whole, like neurons in the brain, conscious of all happenings throughout the Universe. This should not be so hard to accept or understand, seeing that light is the building block of the whole Universe. Even if we look at this from a very linear scientific perspective, life would not be possible without our Sun.

Before we go any further, the term multidimensional planetary system needs explication. We are acquainted with the term planetary system and its meaning. However, this is a linear overview of what's happening in the Universe and in our own backyard. It is said that the microcosm that is man is a reflection of the macrocosm, the Universe. This is absolutely true, and the number seven is vital for this understanding.

There are seven centers of energy/consciousness in man. Similarly, there are seven planes of existence with their own vibratory energy and reflective consciousness. By this statement, you can infer that the "fate" of a "planet" is directly intertwined with the life residing on it and how they evolve over time. Let's put this into parts regarding our own planetary system.

Around our Sun (star), planetary bodies form and revolve around it. They are portions of consciousness/energy that coalesce to create the first potential plane of existence. You should understand that there are seven planes of existence and that they exist potentially within these planetary bodies, not actually. They remain dormant, in a "timeless" state, waiting. Not all planetary bodies have this potential. Notwithstanding, these planets work as instruments for our creative director.

Table 6º - The seven planes or cycles of existence.

Seventh	The Cycle of Ascension (Borderline into the Transcendental)
Sixth	The Cycle of Unity*
Fifth	The Cycle of Wisdom
Forth	The Cycle of Love & Understanding
Third	The Cycle of Self-Awareness
Second	The Cycle of Growth
First	The Cycle of Awakening

Note: There is a correlation with what's expounded in the Hindu scriptures, although not a linear one. There are also places of mystery that I do not depict. The Hindus speak somewhat on this subject, but I do not "completely" grasp their nature, so I feel no real value in addressing it.
* - This Unity relates to Love and Wisdom. They should be as one in balance/harmony.

There are metaphysical planes within these planes of existence, but only from the third plane upward. They go by many names, but we might call them inner planes. These seven planes of existence (Table 6) are the outer crust of our multidimensional Universe, its outward expression, while the inner planes are what lies "within," unseen by most. To use Earth as an example, what we see, be it our bodies or surroundings, is nothing more than the outer crust of our physical plane. The so-called inner planes cannot be accessed by the physical body; only in consciousness and through more subtle bodies. Hindu scripture depicts some of these, and you might want to revisit Table 4, as some of them are outlined in the lower planes.

At a certain point, one of the planetary bodies with such a potential starts to "move." By the action of the upward-spiraling Light, the process of awakening begins, and time starts for that particular planetary sphere. This evolution starts at the mineral level, moving ever so slowly into the first expression of life; at a certain point in time, graduation comes naturally into the second plane of existence—the cycle of Growth. Here we begin with simple single-celled organisms, growing slowly into higher and higher grades of life, from simple plant life to trees, to simple animal life forms, growing ever more complex over time. At a certain point, graduation comes again, and some of these more evolved expressions of life are ready to move on to the next plane of existence, the cycle of Self-Awareness. Here the soul comes into a body that enables it to become self-aware, which in the case of the Earth is man.[32]

These first three planes of existence are all visible to the self-aware entity, for they are the acting playground for their activity. However, the higher planes of existence are veiled from their view and knowledge. As you can see, the evolution of a planetary sphere is directly intertwined with the living entities dwelling within it. They move as one. These primary planes may appear to be one because they are physical, but I assure you they are not. I believe a link between the planes and the bodies they support will help and give an overview of things (see Table 7). However, before doing so, I would like to say that I will use terms and names that are more in line with the universal concept and not in line with any particular religion/philosophy.

---

[32] The human being was indeed a special creation, but this was an exception to the rule. The evolution of life in a particular planetary sphere is usually a "natural" one. A branching out of possibility. At a certain point, life evolves to a higher grade, capable of expressing itself differently, endowed with the free will to choose - the Self-aware. Remember, this does not make man any more special than other sentient life forms in this plane of existence. The body is not important. What really matters are the conscious choices of the souls dwelling within them.

Table 7° - Cycles, body depictions, and examples.

Cycle (Plane)	Cycle	True Sphere Cycle	True Body	Examples
Seventh	The Cycle of Ascension	Violet Energy Cycle	Violet Energy Body	---------
Sixth	The Cycle of Unity	Indigo Energy Cycle	Indigo Energy Body	---------
Fifth	The Cycle of Wisdom	Blue Energy Cycle	Blue Energy Body	---------
Forth	The Cycle of Love & Understanding	Green Energy Cycle	Green Energy Body	---------
Third	The Cycle of Self-Awareness	Yellow Energy Cycle	Yellow Energy Body	Man.
Second	The Cycle of Growth	Orange Energy Cycle	Orange Energy Body	Bacteria, simple plant life, Trees, Insects, Animals...
First	The Cycle of Awakening	Red Energy Cycle	Red Energy Body	Minerals moving to the first bacteria.

Note: Often, the wise of India depict most of the planes above our own (Third) as astral, but this is an oversimplification, a useful one at times but a simplification nevertheless. One might also say that there are several grades of astral, which is not without merit but still far from conveying a deeper understanding of the workings within our material Universe. In a broader sense, all these perspectives are good. The minds that convey these truths always try to give them in a way that accommodates many, usually for a very long time.

In essence, what Table 7 gives is this: The first plane of existence is the red energy cycle. It supports red energy bodies, which are the minerals moving along with other elements to, over a very long period of time, create the first expression of life: bacteria. The second plane of existence is the orange energy cycle. It supports orange energy bodies, which are the various expressions of life moving from one to another in a balanced fashion. Here we begin with simple single-celled organisms, progressing to simple plant life, insects, trees, and so on and so forth, eventually creating the self-aware entity. At such a time, the yellow energy cycle begins (the third plane). Here the playground is set to sustain the Self-aware entity, allowing it to evolve, experience, and express.

The Third Plane - Choice

This plane of existence is key. Here, the self-aware entity is free to experience and choose. In a broader sense, this choice is how one moves toward the Infinite. For a long time, I thought the choice was either turning to God or turning from Him. This was erroneous thinking on my part because there is no possibility of turning from Him since everything is Him and comes from Him. On the other hand, this did not explain what was happening in the world.

I had already set some groundwork on this subject when I spoke of the modes of nature, but I will now expand somewhat. We should first consider the next plane of progression, which is the plane of Love & Understanding. In order to move forward, every entity has to make a choice: **to Love & Understand others or to Love & Understand the self**—the way of the positive or the way of the negative, light or darkness. Understand that this world, this life, is just an opportunity to express one or the other. That is your choice. There's no faking it and no hiding it.[33]

It should become clear that the roles we play are just an opportunity to experience and express light or darkness in different ways and grades. In this world, we experience a wide variety of interpersonal relationships: father, mother, husband, wife, son, daughter, brother, etc. These are important forms of interaction, but so are all others. Jesus Christ came into the world to show the way of the positive in its purest form. He went to great lengths to teach and show the ways of love & understanding for others, even in death. One might say that Jesus was the embodiment of love and understanding, and in a way, he was.

---

[33] To love and understand others is the same as understanding yourself, non-different. Those who love and understand only themselves, see others as less, as tools to be used for their pleasure.

Each cycle has its own center of focus, and in the Cycle of Self-awareness, that center of focus is **choice**. Graduation comes cyclically, every 25,000 years, and only those who choose and learn are fit to enter the next cycle of progression.[34]

As we approached full circle, a great sense of urgency was impressed upon the Universe. As a result, many loving souls came to teach and emphasize the importance of these lessons and that choice. This is why Jesus taught the way he did. This is why he lived. This is why he died. It's important to know that no one expects you to be like Jesus. In time, these lessons will be learned in full in the plane above our own (the Fourth). Understand that perfection is not needed, but expressing, to a certain degree, love and understanding for others is definitely a requirement. Try to love others just a little more than you do yourself. Breaking even might get you close enough, but strive to be consistent. Swinging back and forth will just not do.

In India, the process is seen and taught as a whole, and progression can be attained at any one point in the cycle, but connecting to the One is no easy task, and few succeed in the flicker of a human lifetime. So, to recap: progression can be attained at the end of each cycle or at any one point by establishing the divine connection. Despite all difficulties in the process, a few bright souls have managed to succeed, but it might surprise you to know that a few dark ones did as well.

---

[34] The cycles of the Self-aware are not endless. Quite the opposite. Their length and number might differ from planetary system to planetary system, but emphasis is put on making them "short" (Third Plane).

The Fork in the Road

The path of the negative or of service to self is extremely difficult. Most of these souls linger at the "door" as tools to be used by others. Only very few who are extreme in their service will enter at the end of each cycle. Some of these are even driven enough to connect to the One Consciousness, which is indeed a feat of no small measure.[35]

Now let me make clear that the choice being made does not lead to the very same place. Yes, they do graduate into the plane of Love & Understanding. However, they do not occupy the very same space. Each region of space will reflect the nature of the path chosen by each. One leads to the positive, and the other to the negative. The ones who gain entry into the Fourth negative plane are due for a period of great struggle. Each will try to gain position over every other in order to establish a hierarchy that, in turn, is submitted to a higher one, and so on and so forth. In short, it is just another form of enslavement.

I know these souls are better equipped to learn the lessons of their chosen path, but I nevertheless feel sorry for them. They have no rest, always desiring to gain more and, at the same time, always in fear of losing what they have. Those below are seen as tools or threats, while those above are perceived as controllers, and goals to be taken.

These souls follow the cycles of progression through the ways of the negative, but in time they'll converge into one, for there is no Unity to be found in such a solitary path. At some point, you might have questioned: How are these souls, so negatively driven, able to connect to Infinite Intelligence? The answer is simple: the One sees all as One, each endowed with

---

[35] One such entity was Grigory Rasputin, and his life story left me in a particular state of confusion, longing for answers that would eventually come after some time of distress. If you do not know this character's life story, I strongly advise you to do so. It will give you a greater understanding of what I speak, serving as an example of a certain type.

free will, non-different. As such, each and every one of them has the right to tap or access the same thing. The path might be different, but they all lead to the very same place.[36]

Influence

Light and darkness cast their influence from above, nurturing their ways upon the self-aware, but they are bound by the Law of Free Will. None may come to interfere with the free will of those sitting outside their own plane of existence. As you can imagine, these two forces act very differently in their ways. The forces of light aid those who seek and call, while the forces of darkness act in a somewhat broader spectrum, as they see the law of free will as something to be bent, as a challenge to their creativity and influence.

The negative forces seek out those of like mind, be they calling or not. They use them to create an elite, which in turn enforces the ways of the negative by enslaving, controlling, and manipulating others to their will. This, of course, takes on many forms, from the explicit to the most subtle. One's mind can run wild with this, and any form you can imagine is probably put into action in one way or another (see Appendix III). Many of us live in a daze, conforming to the way of things. We remain unaware that there is even a choice to be made, and for those of the negative, this is just how things should be, our rightful place as it were. However, there are always some who blossom into the light. They become beacons of change for others, which does not sit well for those on the opposite side (negative). As such, these forces cast their influence in any way possible to either buffer that light or snuff it out completely (see Appendix IV).

---

[36] What we call demons are just self-aware entities who have chosen the negative path. We are all the same, part of the same.

Important Observations

As you can see, the ways of evolution are, in general, of a very slow pace. Progression through the different planes of existence has to be made, whether by the positive or the negative. This process can be more or less harmonious, taking more or less time, but make no mistake. The soul's progression from the First to the Seventh takes a very, very long time. The self-aware often see the way of evolution from a physical perspective, but true evolution is a factor of consciousness that comes to express itself materially. This statement comes with different grades and layers of understanding, but what is important to note is that <u>consciousness comes **first**, its expression **later**</u>.

In theory, the self-aware being has the potential to activate all bodies, moving as an inter-dimensional traveler throughout the Universe. However, this is something extremely hard to do, even more so for those who tread without proper guidance. Those of light who long to connect should focus on harmonizing and balancing their centers of consciousness. Without reaching this balance, which is specific to each, there is no possibility of connecting to the One Consciousness. At this point in time, connection to Infinite Intelligence **is not a requirement for graduation**, but it certainly is a way of making sure.

Balance/Healing: Process and Clarification

Balance does not depend on any one thing. It's a product of an overall approach that includes, among other things, how we think, relax, eat, and sleep. However, success may rest on the balance we find within ourselves. To illustrate, I will refer to the awakening experience that set me on my spiritual quest.

It always happened in the same way: I was totally relaxed, sitting comfortably on a couch, then suddenly my gaze was fixed, my eyes unblinking, and my breath started to waver like it was following some kind of strange rhythm. At times the breath stopped. At other times, it remained calm and shallow, and in certain moments air rushed in and out, all of this accompanied by a flow of feelings and sensations. In these moments, memories of past experiences came to mind. All of them had an emotional charge (energy) that was primordially negative—unresolved issues stored in the back of my mind. I came to realize that I was looking at these moments through my higher Self, fully aware of the situation and experiencing it in detail. Suddenly, the negative emotional charge transmuted into peace and joy (bliss), always giving me a newfound understanding of these past experiences.

So, you should first understand that all spiritual/meditative practices aim to bring you closer to your higher Self so that this balance and "healing" may occur. Some might say that balance has nothing to do with healing, but how can the former exist without the latter? How can we balance anything if we are all kinds of broken?

Many things inadvertently keep us from connecting. One of them is misunderstanding who or what God is, His creation, and our connection to Him. But there are others, usually things we keep deep within ourselves. We often run and hide from everything uncomfortable/painful, seeking only that which is pleasurable/agreeable. Running and hiding from these feelings does not solve anything, nor does it help to try to change or "fix" them by force. Only through your higher Self can true emotional and physical healing take place.

Steps and Advice

Don't run or avoid anything. Face what the Universe sends your way. Try not to see anything as good or bad but as an opportunity to learn, experience, merge, and transmute. Watch through your higher Self all thoughts and experiences that come, along with their corresponding emotional energies. Live or relive them as soon as they come, as soon as you can. Try to do so in your meditative practice. It will make the process easier. In time, you will be able to execute this process even while dwelling in very subtle levels of intensity.

My second piece of advice would be to avoid trying to relive any past spiritual experiences. The more you try to do so, the more they fade away, and the more frustrated you'll become. Every experience is unique in its own way, so let go of them and receive whatever comes.

How to do it:

- Put yourself in a higher state of awareness, concentrate, breathe, and relax. There are various ways of doing this: prayer, mantras, visualization, breathing techniques, etc. Some use a combination of these, and others use all, but if I had to choose one out of the rest, it would be breathing (breathwork). As you become more proficient, you will find that you'll need to use these techniques less and less. One day, you'll find that you need them no more.

- Experience whatever comes. Try to bring forth unresolved issues and emotions. Don't run away from anything, even your aches and pains. The more you fight or avoid them, the more they tend to linger and persist.

- Do not judge. If you do so, you'll be taking yourself out of that higher state of awareness, and your mind will go on forever, taking you absolutely nowhere. When you judge, you automatically pass sentence. You confine and bind. Oddly enough, you do it to yourself. When you strive to understand, you cultivate peace and harmony, opening yourself up to giving and receiving.

- Be aware, and tune in to the feelings that come with any thought/situation. Experience in "detail" but without "focus." What I mean is this: if you're looking at a cube, don't focus on its parts, like its edge or its color. Be in a place of full awareness where you can take it all in. See everything that makes up the cube, all its qualities, the environment it's in, its interactions with the environment, observe from different perspectives, etc. This is not a mechanical process. This is how your higher Self sees. You just have to let it.

Whatever comes, whatever you feel, be sure to know that it's OK, nobody is judging you, and more importantly, you are not judging yourself. When you're able to do these things to some extent, you'll feel, at times, something moving within you, and I say this literally. Masters often serve as mirrors in this process, which is usually a difficult one, but you can do it yourself if you are truly earnest about it.

There are many on the spiritual path that state they have no need for a spiritual master, and I have to say that it is true that we now live in an age where some spiritual independence is possible. Still, even if you do not believe in the need for such things, you will inadvertently find that you'll have many teachers in your life and that some will hold a more prominent position in your heart than others, whether you call them master or not. Mind you that I'm not advocating blind loyalty to anyone or anything. Do not use this concept as an excuse to act blindly, mindlessly disregarding the nature of what's being said and done. We're not robots, so try to refrain from acting like one (see Appendix V).

My Final Thoughts

On the spiritual path, I often heard many quoting scripture, the masters, Jesus, and others. These quotations were often extensive and detailed, which always took me aback. Not that there was anything wrong with conveying the wisdom expounded by others, but because I sensed a feeling of security and contentment in those who were doing so. First of all, Truth stands on its own two feet. It needs no backing from any individual personality or scripture, and if you're receptive, you'll perceive it either coming from others or from within yourself. It is true that we need a strong and reliable foundation of knowledge/wisdom in our spiritual path, which is usually given by a Guru, Teacher, Saint, etc. Still, this is just the groundwork.

Do not get stuck on any particular personality, for they are not the goal. I love and respect all these compassionate souls. I am truly grateful for their mission in "life" and beyond it, but how often have you seen the student surpass the master? This is no fault of the teacher, for he or she cares for nothing more than the true happiness and development of others. They are not bound by egotistic emotions of being greater or lesser than others. The fault lies within you, within us. Aren't we supposed to be growing as a whole into higher states of consciousness, and higher states of being? When you condition your growth in this way, you condition the growth of the whole (of humanity).

Some are content in knowing the One just a little. Others would say they know enough, and a few will think (and perhaps not say) that they know a lot. However, these are material constructs. What is a lot? What is a little? For those living in higher planes of existence or consciousness, these concepts would have a completely different meaning—or no meaning at all.

I was often told by the powers that be that the need for confirmation was OK in the beginning but ultimately dangerous. I was told to be humble but also to stop being so humble. This, of course, left me confounded for a long time, but I came to understand it. I had to surrender. Trust in what I've been given and ultimately share it with others if and when I can. I will always strive to nurture a deeper connection with the One, and I advise you to do the same. Contentment is, in a sense, the enemy of the soul's progress, and it will ultimately lead you nowhere. Here I speak spiritually, of course, for we should always strive to find material contentment in life.

I'll leave you with this, we are all individualized expressions of the One. We all have something to give, in our own little way, so try not to pose as any other, be them masters, prophets, saints, Jesus, or anyone else, just be your own perfect "little" Self.

The Life and Spiritual Journey of No One

Conclusion

This whole book was a process of unraveling, just as much as it was a process of unraveling myself. There are no mistakes and no coincidences. We just have to be mindful of what is happening inwardly and outwardly. The forces of light never fail to give a helping hand. We only need to be open enough to grasp it. My life and how this book came into being are ample proof of that: events, spiritual phenomena, experiences, books, dreams, visions, memories, realizations—bits and pieces of past, present, and future coming together as one. I evolved from a state of doubt, pain, and fear to a state of trust, peace, understanding, and love. I was born with erroneous concepts and notions that obstructed my sight, but these gradually unraveled and dissolved into newfound wisdom and understanding.

On this path, I've struggled with every little thing one might struggle with, but may my struggles ease your own, whatever they may be. I didn't overcome anything on my own, as you may have realized. I was helped in many different ways and forms, so I hope this book becomes one of the ways to help you too.

Ever since I was little, I felt that true love was not of this world, but even though I felt it, I never stopped looking. I cautiously strove to find it, to see it in others, but time only aided in placing the heavy weight of failure down on my shoulders. It all seemed like nothing more than fiction. It's true that we live in a complicated world, and we should always be mindful of that, but instead of striving to find love, shouldn't we just focus on bringing it into the world in whatever measure we can? Maybe that's all we need to do; all we need to do.

Author's Note

Your Insights Are Invaluable

Dear Reader,

As this literary and spiritual journey concludes, I sincerely hope that this book has played a role in your life's unfolding. Becoming an author was not in my plans; it emerged as a response to a greater force compelling me to share its contents. Though feeling somewhat unequipped for this task, I embarked on this duty-driven quest.

Recognizing the enormity of this venture, I turn to you, the reader, with a humble request. If you believe this book has touched you, and its message is worth sharing with the world, I invite you to take a moment to craft an honest review. Your insights hold significant value, and I would be deeply honored by your feedback on platforms like Goodreads and any other site of your choosing. Your thoughts can indeed make a meaningful difference.

Thank you for sharing your time. Should you have any questions or thoughts to share directly, please feel free to reach out.

Warm regards,

R. J. Fidalgo

New Book:

Earth, The Improbable Utopia

Note: I never intended to do a follow up on "The life and Spiritual Journey of No One". However, events led me to write a book that turned out to be a very natural sequel to the first. This book, much like the first, is pretty out of the norm, but I hope it might be an important tool someday.

You can reach out to me via this site:

Your Journey of Life

www.yourjol.com

The Life and Spiritual Journey of No One

Appendix I

Dementia – The Broken Complex

The human entity is a complex of body, mind, and spirit. These elements make up a working unit that enables each individual to express themselves in life. However, certain forms of disease or injury might come to condition an entity in its endeavors. Those with strong wills may come to "succeed" in life despite physical disabilities, but things might turn out quite different when it comes to the mind. Both my mother and mother-in-law have been going through difficult stages of dementia with no real prospects of getting better. My mother-in-law's dementia was a more in-your-face problem since we took her in at a certain point. However, despite finding it physically and mentally difficult to handle, my mother's state was emotionally harder.

Daily life with my mother-in-law is difficult, but she still responds to stimuli even in her state. She's unable to do anything by herself, but somehow we manage to arrange fleeting moments of joy and mental comfort. Nights are somewhat more challenging: she moves about often in the wee hours of the night, moving stuff, talking loudly, turning on lights, etc. She keeps doing things with no clear intent or direction. So many times, I put her to sleep only to see her move about just seconds later. Often, I lead her to the bathroom only to see her walk out almost immediately. Something new always seems to come, and not in a positive way. Without going into specifics, I believe some of you can understand how physically and mentally challenging this is.

My mother's case is somewhat different. She was living at home and seemed to be displaying lighter and more manageable symptoms of the condition. However, things suddenly worsened, leading my father to place her in a nursing home. The first time I saw her there, it came as a bit of a shock. What a frail and innocent presence. Nothing seems to move her, only fleeting sad memories from long ago, which weigh heavily on me. The only real comfort she wants and needs is not to be alone. Such experiences have made me realize that once the mind is gone, the complex is broken, and life just drags out.

I began feeling somewhat frustrated. Here I was, surrounded by people whom I'm unable to "help" for a number of different reasons. Yes, I do things for them, and this doing springs out of love, which is right in itself, but if these actions do not move to grow something good within them, what is their "true" worth? Forgive my digressions. This just seems like the right place to express some of my frustrations at the time; I was seeking a higher form of service, but it all seemed so far from me.

Appendix II

Acts of Kindness/Helping Others

Those on the spiritual path are often set on helping others, on doing good. However, most of the time, things end up going sideways. It's always important to ascertain the receptiveness of those you are trying to help and if they perceive your actions as helpful or good. If they do not, it is better to step back, wish them well, and love them from afar. Like in so many other things, there are exceptions to this, and parenting is one of them. Parents should always establish rules and some degree of "discipline" for the benefit of their children, but children rarely see these acts as good or helpful. One could and should explain the reasoning behind them, but often enough, their perception remains the same.

Now speaking to those on the receiving end: Please do not scorn or disregard any true act of kindness, even if you feel it is misplaced. See it for what it is: an expression of love. Greet such acts with affection even if you intend to courteously "reject" them. Acts of love and virtue need no recognition, for they are right in themselves. However, I feel there is an urgent need in this world to nurture them, and I speak of the little things, like saying "Thank You," giving a kind smile, a heartfelt handshake, a warm embrace, etc. Whatever suits the occasion, they are worth more than you think.

The Life and Spiritual Journey of No One

Appendix III

War on Ukraine

It's not my intent to dwell on negative expressions, be they light or not. However, there was an event in 2022 with such global repercussions that many would feel it was amiss on my part not to speak of it. On the 24th of February 2022, Russian military forces began an incursion into Ukrainian territory, ultimately leading to a war that came to affect the whole world. War is a negative expression that branches out into many forms. Speaking of it would lead to a far too extensive book, which is not my intent nor the purpose of this book. In war, both sides think of themselves as being "right," and they strive to sell that idea to their people and the world.

There is only one true and complete story, and only very few are really privy to it. Winners, if we can call them that, tend to write history however they want, especially to their people. Russian forces call themselves liberators, but I am pretty sure that the Ukrainian people don't see it that way. The purpose of this small exposition is not to lift up or drag down any one party. Those on a path of goodness should be able to "see" and understand the true nature (positive/negative) of what is being said and done without any form of bias, be it based on race, country/nation, religion, or political position. Light and darkness can claim "righteousness" as their own, but you should come to a place where no one, not even a master, should need to tell you the true nature (positive/negative) of whatever you are facing. Acquiring this state of discernment is more important than labeling things as "wrong" or "right." Getting there might take some time, but I hope this book helps you get there a little faster.

The Life and Spiritual Journey of No One

Appendix IV

Attempt on my life

I might say that there were many attempts in the works, but one of them came into effect. Despite failing its primary purpose, it did not fail to leave me with an emotional scar. I was about 15 or 16 years of age at the time, and as I was pretty fond of playing football, I would often take any recess at school as an opportunity to play. One day, a childish dispute over play drove a friend to toss me to the ground. I immediately reversed the situation, ending up on the ground on top of him. As I was about to punch him to make a point, I felt a powerful jolt to my head, which sent me flying quite a distance. Somehow, I ended up standing, realizing I'd just received a kick to the temple delivered at full force with the tip of a tennis shoe. That was about it as we stood at a standstill. I was too stunned to do anything against two opponents, and they were too surprised to see me standing, apparently ready for anything. The next morning, I seemed pretty OK. The exception would be a small round bruise on my right temple that eventually disappeared after a few days.

I was physically fine, but the event did manage to make an enduring mark on me. Whenever I thought about it, I got so angry and didn't know why. I've been hurt many times before and never felt this way about other instances. Was this due to the sneaky nature of the attack? No. What left me so angry was the total disregard for human life. I was just a thing, an object, no better than a ball. He was probably more affectionate towards a ball.

I realize now that I often felt that very same way every time I saw blatant expressions of disregard for life, but this is just another way of falling under the negative influence. Feelings like fear and anger will inadvertently bind you if you let them. I realize the reasons behind these actions and feel nothing but compassion for those who are suffering and for those who are inflicting it, for very often, they will find themselves in that very same spot.

Appendix V

Loyalty to a Master

Those who know the story of Paramahansa Yogananda should realize that his relationship with his Guru (Yukteswar) was not one of blind loyalty. His connection to Master Yukteswar was nurtured by years of pure expressions, words, and actions—a relationship of real affection, unconditioned by self-interest. If you recall, Paramahansa Yogananda left his master's ashram after six months of being there. Did his master consider him a traitor? No, he welcomed him with open arms.

Now, what if P. Yogananda chose differently? What if he decided to live in the Himalayas instead of returning? Would his master's demeanor remain the same, or would he consider him a traitor? The answer should be obvious. Master Yukteswar never refrained from sharing his wisdom; at the same time, he never strove to bind others with it. He encouraged his disciples to have their own perceptions and realizations—to grow and not to be bound by anything.

It is essential, in the beginning, to establish fertile ground in the seeker's mind. This is a challenging endeavor at times, but it is made smoother by the instruction of a more enlightened mind—a Guru, as he is called in India. This groundwork will set the seeker on a journey of their own. Alone and bound by no one, and that is, and should be, the real purpose of a true teacher. The real Guru is the Divine that "lives" within us all, and if you allow it, you will come to become both master and disciple.

The Life and Spiritual Journey of No One

Bibliography

Krajčovičová-Kudláčková, M., et al. "Iodine Deficiency in Vegetarians and Vegans." Annals of Nutrition and Metabolism, vol. 47, no. 5, S. Karger AG, 2003, pp. 183–85. https://doi.org/10.1159/000070483.

Daas, M. C., and N. M. de Roos. "Intermittent Fasting Contributes to Aligned Circadian Rhythms Through Interactions With the Gut Microbiome." *Beneficial Microbes*, vol. 12, no. 2, Wageningen Academic Publishers, Apr. 2021, pp. 147–61. https://doi.org/10.3920/bm2020.0149.

Mohr, Alex E., et al. "Recent Advances and Health Implications of Dietary Fasting Regimens on the Gut Microbiome." *American Journal of Physiology-Gastrointestinal and Liver Physiology*, vol. 320, no. 5, American Physiological Society, May 2021, pp. G847–63. https://doi.org/10.1152/ajpgi.00475.2020.

Palmer, Biff F., and Deborah J. Clegg. "Metabolic Flexibility and Its Impact on Health Outcomes." *Mayo Clinic Proceedings*, vol. 97, no. 4, Elsevier BV, Apr. 2022, pp. 761–76. https://doi.org/10.1016/j.mayocp.2022.01.012.

Pereira, Thiago M. C., et al. "The Emerging Scenario of the Gut–Brain Axis: The Therapeutic Actions of the New Actor Kefir Against Neurodegenerative Diseases." *Antioxidants*, vol. 10, no. 11, MDPI AG, Nov. 2021, p. 1845. https://doi.org/10.3390/antiox10111845.

Vieira, Carla P., et al. "Bioactive Compounds From Kefir and Their Potential Benefits on Health: A Systematic Review and Meta-Analysis." *Oxidative Medicine and Cellular Longevity*, edited by Demetrios Kouretas, vol. 2021, Hindawi Limited, Oct. 2021, pp. 1–34. https://doi.org/10.1155/2021/9081738.

Li, Linghao, et al. "The Effects of Daily Fasting Hours on Shaping Gut Microbiota in Mice." *BMC Microbiology*, vol. 20, no. 1, Springer Science and Business Media LLC, Mar. 2020, https://doi.org/10.1186/s12866-020-01754-2.

Vyāsadeva. *The Song Celestial, or Bhagavad-Gita (From the Mahabharata)*. Translated by Edwin Arnold, 2000. *Project Gutenberg*, www.gutenberg.org.

Dharma, Krishna. *Mahabharata: The Greatest Spiritual Epic of All Time*. Torchlight Publishing, 1999.

Vyāsadeva. *S'rîmad Bhâgavatam*. Translated by Anand Aadhar, 3rd ed., vol. 12, 2020, www.srimadbhagavatam.org.

Griffith, Ralph. *The Rámáyan of Válmíki: Translated Into English Verse*. 2008. *Project Gutenberg*, www.gutenberg.org.

Shastri, Hari Prasad. *The Ramayana of Valmiki*. 1952. Isha Books, www.wisdomlib.org/hinduism/book/the-ramayana-of-valmiki.

Wilson, Horace Hayman. *The Vishnu Purana*. 1840. 1.0, Oxford, United Kingdom of Great Britain and Northern Ireland, John Murray, Albemarle Street.

Prabhupada, Swami Bhaktivedanta, et al. *Sri Caitanya-caritamrta, Adi-lila*. The Bhaktivedanta Book Trust, 2012.

Prabhupada, Swami Bhaktivedanta, et al. *Sri Caitanya-caritamrta, Madhya-lila*. The Bhaktivedanta Book Trust, 2012.

Prabhupada, Swami Bhaktivedanta, et al. *Sri Caitanya-caritamrta, Antya-lila*. The Bhaktivedanta Book Trust, 2012.

The Holy Bible: King James Version. 1611. King's Printer, www.holybooks.com.